LOST PORTSMOUTH

R. J. COOK & K. C. CLOSE

Acknowledgements

Images

Portsmouth City Museum & Library
Portsmouth News
Simmons Aerofilms
Authors' Work & Collections

The authors wish to thank all of those people interviewed and mentioned in the text, as well as so many more who have informed and assisted us with our research and photography over the years.

First published 2022

Amberley Publishing
The Hill, Stroud
Gloucestershire, GL5 4EP

www.amberley-books.com

Copyright © R. J. Cook & K. C. Close, 2022

The right of R. J. Cook & K. C. Close to be identified as the Authors of this work has been asserted in accordance with the Copyrights, Designs and Patents Act 1988.

All rights reserved. No part of this book may be reprinted or reproduced or utilised in any form or by any electronic, mechanical or other means, now known or hereafter invented, including photocopying and recording, or in any information storage or retrieval system, without the permission in writing from the Publishers.

British Library Cataloguing in Publication Data.

A catalogue record for this book is available from the British Library.

ISBN 978 1 4456 9903 5 (print)
ISBN 978 1 4456 9904 2 (ebook)

Typesetting by SJmagic DESIGN SERVICES, India.
Printed in the UK.

Contents

Introduction 4

1 Shore Enough 10

2 Icons 14

3 Naval Gazing 19

4 Heaven and Hell 31

5 Seaside 38

6 Tricorn Haze 51

7 In Dock 59

8 Power and Glory 66

9 Byways 73

10 Community 81

11 Where Now? 90

Introduction

The Collins Dictionary shows us that the word 'lost' means 'Unable to be found or recovered, unable to find one's whereabouts, confused, bewildered or helpless'.

In this context, asked about Portsmouth's greatest loss, many people told us it was the sense of community. Community goes hand in hand with a feeling of belonging. That community had been forged through centuries of hardship, tragedy, suffering, customs and culture handed down. Hardship for many endures. Religion was comfort for many, as was drink for the non-believers who could afford it. There were 305 alehouses and 372 beerhouses in the Portsmouth of 1915.

The Second World War killed many people, destroying tightly packed slums, businesses and places of worship in the process. Evacuation and call-up to service reduced the city's pre-war population from 260,000 to 136,000 by September 1941. Portsmouth was a prime military target, and civilians were reduced to what is called collateral damage.

Portsmouth is Britain's only island city, and the only city in the UK to exceed London's population density. Historically, it had four gates through strong walls and fortifications. Of these, Landport Gate is the only one that remains where it was first built. King James Gate used to guard entry into the then dangerous Broad Street and The Point, in 1687. It now guards entry to the United Services Sports Ground.

The island is an administrative area of a mere 23.2 square miles (the land area is only 15.5 square miles), but an awful lot has been packed in over centuries of expansion north and east from the original harbour area. William the Conqueror's Domesday Census of 1086 registered only thirty-one households on Portsea Island. The 2011 census recorded a population of 205,100. It is home to two-thirds of the UK's naval fleet – a key factor in the city's rise. Naval cuts have been a major force behind change, loss and impact on local culture.

Significant reference to mass culture began during the Second World War, with the Mass Observation organisation continuing into the post-war years. Cinema took over from music halls and theatre. Television was stalled by war, but computers were already doing the business at Bletchley Park. War was Portsmouth's business. The 1939–45 horror changed Portsmouth forever. It was a sea change for the world.

Improved mass education and health care were priorities when planning for peace. Youth was going to be indulged, though young males still faced the ordeal of National Service in dangerous conflict zones for years to come.

But by the late 1950s, sociologists were talking about youth culture, respecting the jobs boom and youth spending power. As Britain's leaders looked towards reconstruction, there was a new interest in social progress and caring for the young. Technology made all sorts of things possible – and the age of consumerism was born. Young working-class people were eager to leave school, to earn and spend.

However, Britain had the expensive difficulty of withdrawing from an empire that had been shaken to pieces by the all-consuming nightmare of the Second World War. As Britain's premier naval base, the Royal Dockyard, and home of the Royal Marines, Portsmouth would be heavily impacted over the next decades of rapid economic and social change. Post-war penny pinching was such that rather than spend £500,000 in 1949 to restore the world's oldest wooden warship, HMS *Implacable* (captured from the French at Trafalgar), the vessel was scuttled in the Channel, though the figurehead was preserved at Greenwich. As the dockyard declined, so the university has expanded to fill the void.

Only a few feet separate the increasingly densely populated Portsea Island from the English mainland. Hayling to the east is a little further offshore. The chalk South Downs form a barrier to the north. Drainage was a challenge in both Portsea and Hayling – with Langstone Harbour between them. Waste water had nowhere to go.

Bad drainage harboured disease. Before Portsmouth's first drainage scheme in 1851, twenty-five out of every 1,000 people died of disease, especially cholera, because of stagnant water. In 1858, the borough bought Havant springs, building a new pumping station at Bedhampton. An improved water supply meant safer beer, among other things.

The Borough Engineer submitted plans for underground sewers with outfall into Langstone Harbour. Because the land was so flat and boggy, Eastney Pumping Station was built using two Clayton Steam pumping engines to accelerate disposal. In spite of all the best efforts towards land reclamation, increasing development and worsening storms mean that flooding remains a challenge. Water has been a problem for so long that the first telephone line connected Portsmouth Waterworks to the police station at Landport. Communications were advancing all around, making Portsmouth's landmark semaphore house redundant.

These difficulties explain to a large degree why the Romans never got closer than Portchester. However, evidence of settlement on the island dates back to AD 900. Population was growing, with the area's success down to a fine natural harbour. This wonder of nature was formed by the drowned estuary of the River Wallington, flowing via Fareham Lake. Regardless of tide, there is deep water in the approaches, with the Isle of Wight providing shelter.

Originally, Portsmouth developed around Portsmouth Point, on Portsea Island, facing south-west across the harbour to Gosport. A trading community was established, and Richard I granted the first charter for a market and fairs in 1194. The dockyard was founded in 1212, defining the town's path to growth and progress over many years to come. Henry VII founded 'His Majesty's Nave Royall'.

Fortifications were a priority, with Portsmouth having endured serious raids during the Hundred Years' War. However, it is important to note that Portsmouth was first and foremost a garrison town, becoming home to the Royal Marines, many of whom perished on Henry VIII's ill-fated top-heavy flagship *Mary Rose*, which sank in 1545 during an attempted invasion of France.

For all of the progress over the last century, poverty has been an enduring source of misery in this crowded little island. This has never shaken Portsmouth's loyalty to the Crown. Queen Victoria frequently travelled through Portsmouth en route to her favourite home, Osborne House on the Isle of Wight. A statue commemorates the grand old lady outside the equally grand city council offices.

Portsmouth was inevitably Royalist during the English Civil War, under Governor George Goring, when Parliamentary forces captured Southsea Castle on 4 September 1641.

As Robert Cook wrote in his book *Past and Present: The Changing Face of Portsmouth & Its People* (2002), 'Victorian England was a time of great innovation and ingenuity and there were some great social reformers associated with the town, including Charles Dickens and local newspaper editor W. G. Yates. The lot of ordinary people gradually improved, and the days when individuals could be transported to Botany Bay for minor offences faded into distant memory.'

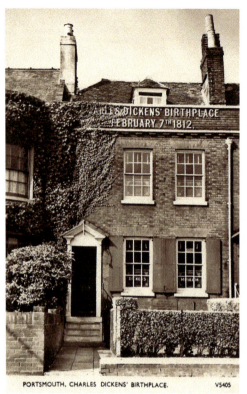

PORTSMOUTH, CHARLES DICKENS' BIRTHPLACE.   V5405

Left: Portsmouth has some interesting literary and artistic claims to fame, including Sir Arthur Conan Doyle, the creator of Sherlock Holmes, and Peter Sellers. There is perhaps none more noteworthy than Charles Dickens. This was his birthplace, in Old Commercial Road, 7 February 1812.

Below: Southsea castle was built in six months in 1544. The land behind was marsh, on which there were multiple gun positions. England had many enemies following the breach with Rome, especially with Henry VIII selling church property to his cronies, using much of the funds to build fortifications. Old Portsmouth's forbidding Round Tower still stands, though mostly rebuilt in the nineteenth century. The Parliamentarians destroyed much of the castle during the English Civil War. Fortifications were an enduring theme up until the age of Lord Palmerston, with offshore forts and Palmerston's so-called 'follies' on Portsdown Hill.

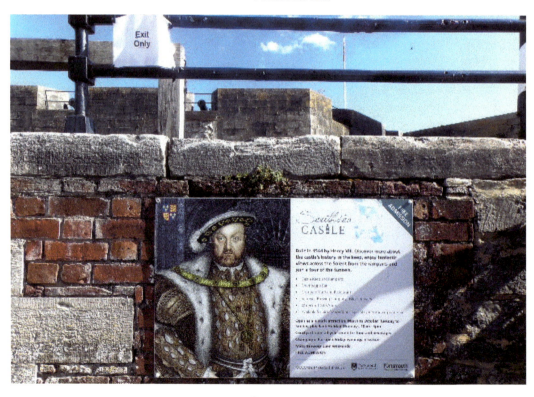

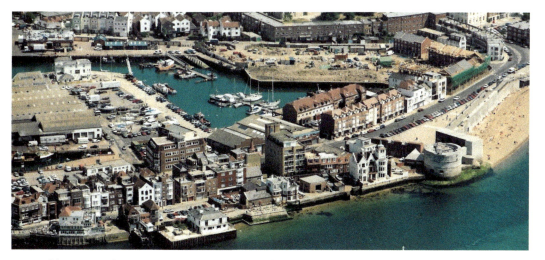

Old Portsmouth, 1995. Quebec House, originally a bathing house and now owned by John Pounds, is among some distinctive properties. Inner Camber is seen busy with boats, while demolition and new building are changing the nature of this once impoverished area, nicknamed Spice Island. Luxury apartments and boating define the locality now. The old Tudor Round Tower has been rebuilt so much that it is mainly Victorian. Admirals, including Lord Nelson, took their carriages along Broad Street, Old Portsmouth, to their ships anchored off 'The Point'. (Simmons Aerofilms)

One must mention the stoic work of the Revd Father Thomas Dolling. He came to Portsmouth on 29 September 1885, appointed to St Agatha's by the Bishop of Winchester. His Portsmouth memoir is entitled *Ten Years in a Portsmouth Slum*. The manner, language and drinking habits of the common folk shocked him. He tried his best to teach them that their salvation was in praising the Lord God Almighty.

Father Dolling described the town as comprising four separate settlements: Portsmouth, thronging with soldiers; Portsea, home to sailors; Southsea, into which the town burst when the moats were removed; and Landport to the north, home to dockyard apprentices. Well, two world wars and politicians have changed much of that. There has been loss, but not all bad.

The words British Empire have unacceptable connotations nowadays, with a growing clamour to tear down or deface statues, of which there is an abundance in Victoria Park. Two world wars had much to do with empire, which brought death and hell to Portsmouth, a prime target. Leaders and people across the nation hoped for better tomorrows, but life will never be that simple.

For many years, Portsmouth – which earned city status and a cathedral in 1926 – the 1920s and 1930s experienced more defence cuts and hardship, which was relieved only by massive rearmament, forces recruitment and preparation for war in 1939. It took until 1998 before a cathedral extension was completed, according to Michael Drury's designs.

Post-war 'baby boomers' were the first to enjoy pop culture and youthful hedonism. To relieve a housing shortage that had been caused by wartime bombing, people were moved to neighbouring little towns, most notably Havant, where new industries were planted. They lived in new quick-build homes.

Portsmouth's Brutalist concrete Tricorn Centre was built by young innovative architects Owen Luder & Rodney Gordon Partnership, on the hellfire triangle of land that had been bombed out as German planes lined up, dropping bombs and range-finding, just short of the neighbouring dockyard.

With its bars and nightclub, The Tricorn was seemingly a concrete display of that new optimism when it opened in 1966, but it soon began to decline, becoming symbolic of a dwindling naval

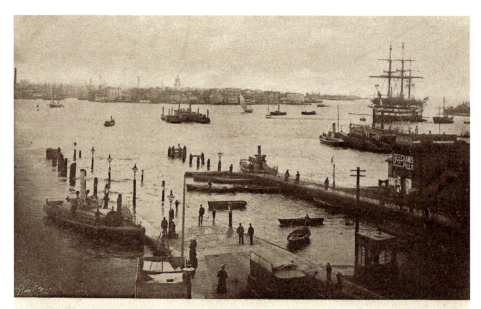

PORTSMOUTH HARBOUR FROM GOSPORT. *Russell & Sons, Photo, Southsea.*

The Chain Ferry midstream is plying its way across the harbour from Gosport to Portsmouth in this early twentieth-century view. The chain ferry began operating in 1840 with the 100-foot by 60-foot *Victoria* followed by the *Albert* in 1842. Earlier, watermen used to row people across the harbour in small boats. With so much demand to move from workers crossing the water to the dockyard, together with the tourist trade to the Isle of Wight, there were soon ferry boats – the so-called V ferries: *Vadne*, *Varos*, *Vesta* and *Vita*.

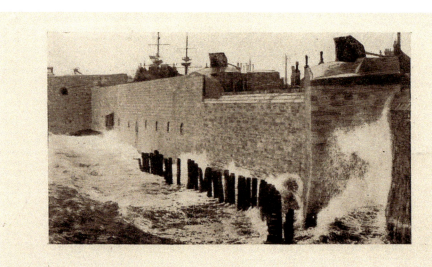

"SALLY PORT," THE POINT BATTERIES U70/1831

Defences have been a Portsmouth preoccupation since turbulent Tudor times. Here are the Sally Port Point Batteries, early twentieth century. On 13 May, what Aussies called the 'first fleet' of eleven slow old ships – six for convicts, two naval and three supply – left from near here for Botany Bay. The 8,000-mile voyage took eight months. Convicted of trying to get food in a rich man's country, these poor white people were aged from thirteen to eighty-two.

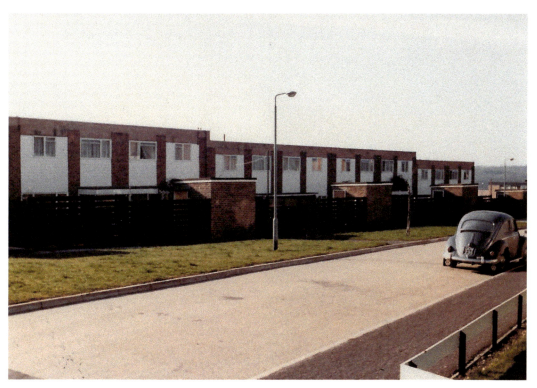

Sandleford Road, Leigh Park, Havant, 1975. This was the home road of local tax man Vernon Church, who migrated down from London as tax work was moved out to centres in the south. Portsmouth City Council purchased the Leigh Park estate for post-war housing, moving bombed-out families away from the city. R. J. Cook lived here in the mid-1970s. (V. F. Church)

town and a diminishing empire. By the 1990s, much of the complex was decaying, soon becoming home to drug users and homeless people.

The city had been struggling to find a new identity from the mid-1970s. As the dockyard's work contracted, the polytechnic became one of Thatcher's new universities, the city council seeing this as symbolising new hope. That hope has been fragile, with 2020's Covid-19 lockdowns adding to the difficulties being experienced by struggling Commercial Road and Palmerston Road. Drug addiction, family break-ups, homelessness, consequent mental health issues and crime have presented great problems.

The university's students have bright futures, perhaps, and can they afford the plethora of new student apartments. This is the age of student loans, with concerns that youngsters will see less purpose in signing up to the expense. The less well educated and hard to employ have even less hope, relying on various charity shops and food banks as Covid-19-related homelessness and unemployment sky rocket. These problems are not peculiar to Portsmouth.

Higher rents have meant inevitable shop closures. Debenhams and Knight and Lee were major landmarks and employers in Palmerston Road. Both have closed, with the site up for a £7.5 million mainly residential development at the time of writing (2020). Life has always been uncertain. That hasn't changed.

Charles Close and R. J. Cook, September 2020

I
Shore Enough

Life on board sailing ships was hard, with discipline harsh. It must have been a great relief when sailors caught sight of their home port of Portsmouth. However, they did not always make the safety of the Portsmouth shore. One miraculous return was that of Captain Bligh and eighteen trusty men, who were set adrift in a longboat after Lieutenant Fletcher Christian led a mutiny against Bligh's harsh discipline. Bligh had been sent from Portsmouth to move breadfruit from Tahiti to the West Indies in 1789. A distinguished navigator who served with Captain James Cook, he navigated 4,000 miles to Timor in the Dutch East Indies, then took ship to England.

HMS *Eurydice*'s crew, under the command of devout Captain Hare, were not so fortunate when returning from Bermuda to Portsmouth on 13 November 1877. A Guildford vicar was apparently seized with a vision of a ship sailing into a storm near the Isle of Wight, then floundering, with all its portholes open. All but two of the 319 crew, including Captain Hare and trainees, drowned. Prince Edward claimed to have seen the ship's ghost. Worse was to come during the Second World War.

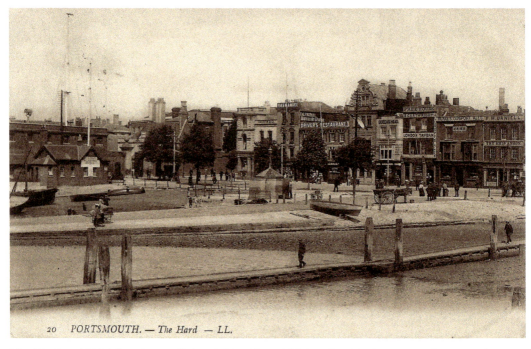

The Hard, *c.* 1908. There is very little of this old world left today. Hard was a perfect name for this place and the times. Notorious for having many pubs, drunks and prostitutes, there were moral campaigns to clean it up. Some called this place 'The Devil's Acre'. Poverty was extreme. Visitors tossed coins into the mud so children, nicknamed 'mudlarks', would dive in head first to retrieve them.

Here land reaches what is called The Point, also known as Spice Island. The name possibly referred to the smell of spices being unloaded or to the spicier side of life on The Point. The area was separated from the town by King James's Gate and filled with eating houses, cook shops, all-day drinking establishments – half of them were crammed in here – pawnshops, brothels, tailors and all manner of services, fulfilling the needs of those who had business with the sea. This early 1970s image shows the docks still busy, with the Isle of Wight car ferry unloading. (Simmons Aerofilms)

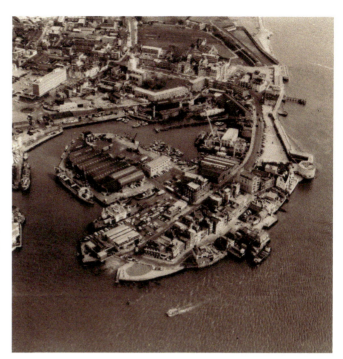

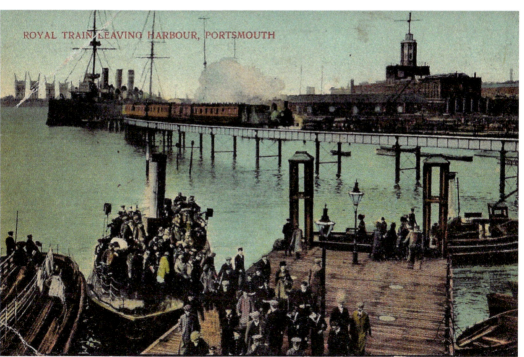

Portsmouth Harbour Station, summertime *c.* 1911. The royal train is coupled to a shunting engine on the fragile-looking pier. Royalty had favoured Portsmouth as a departure point across the Solent since Queen Victoria and her beloved Prince Albert had discovered the wonders of the Isle of Wight. One of the V steamer ferries is unloading happy holidaymakers in the foreground.

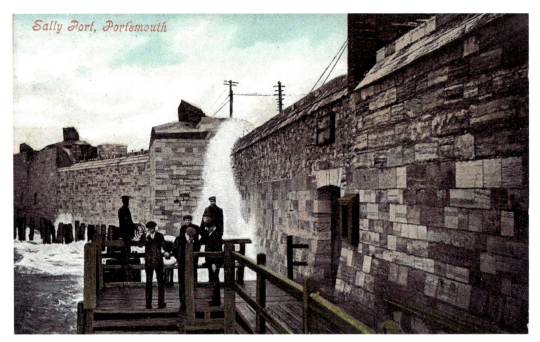

The Sally Port, where the first convict ships were crowded with 780 starving disease-ridden wretches, nearly 600 male and 200 female, separated from their families. Dorothy Hudson was amongst them; she was believed to be the first suicide in Australia.

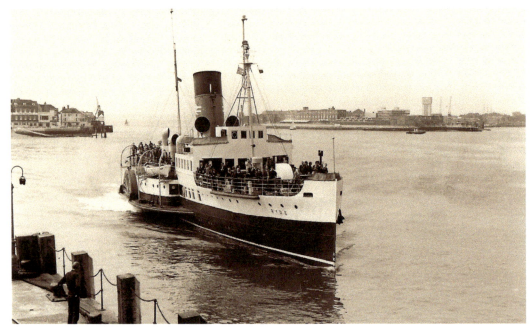

The paddle steamer *Ryde* arriving at Portsmouth, 8 June 1969, its final year of service. It worked between Portmouth and Ryde from 1937, and was then requisitioned by the Royal Navy during the Second World War. After life as an Isle of Wight nightclub, the steamer was found rotting on the banks of the River Medina. Although a restoration was crowdfunded, it proved beyond repair. (Edwin Wilmshurst)

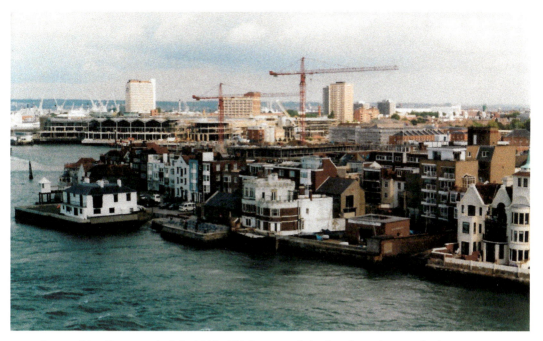

Approaching Portsmouth, July 2002. Old Portsmouth landmarks make way for luxury apartments. Gunwharf's controversial mixed residential and retail development is advancing. By November 2003, Gunwharf Quays had broken the £2 million mark for retail sales in one week.

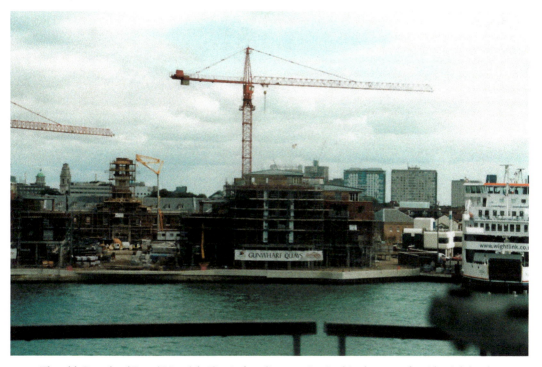

The old Gunwharf Royal Naval facility is fast disappearing in this close-up of residential development, September 2001.

2

Icons

Every age has its heroes and icons – Portsmouth's best known is HMS *Victory* and the Royal Dockyard. There are also landmarks and everyday sights that are or were uniquely Portsmouth.

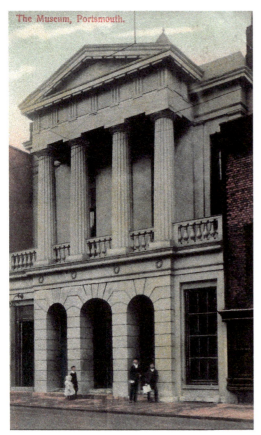 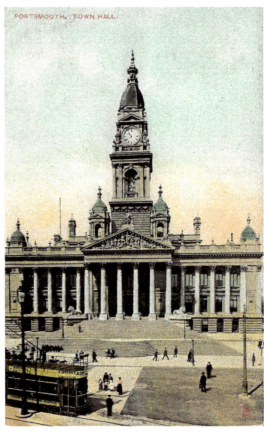

Above left: The Doric-style town hall in Old Portsmouth High Street, in the year of Portsmouth's much-loved Queen Victoria's coronation, 1838. Completed the year after the foundation stone had been laid, it became the town museum when the new town hall opened in 1890. After the building was severely damaged by wartime bombing, a cash-strapped council opted for demolition.

Above right: The new town hall cost £137,098 to build. It is viewed here from the junction of the part of the original Commercial Road that was renamed Guildhall Walk with Russell Street.

The town hall was renamed the Guildhall after city status was granted in 1926. PC Ken Hampton was on duty on 10 January 1941. He recalled that incendiary bombs on the building's roof went unnoticed. A furious fire took hold. He said: 'It was only a couple of incendiaries which went through the ventilator. We were on the roof fire watching, but couldn't locate them. All we could do was watch it burn because we didn't have any water.' Here is the result, photographed in 1951. Looking along what is now Guildhall Walk, there are the remains of the old Hippodrome, the Apollo Kinematic Theatre and the Theatre Royal, which experienced two fires in its history.

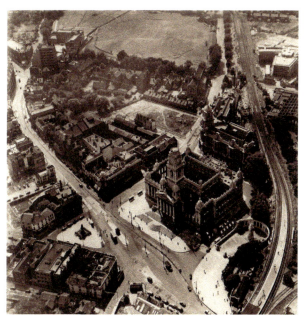

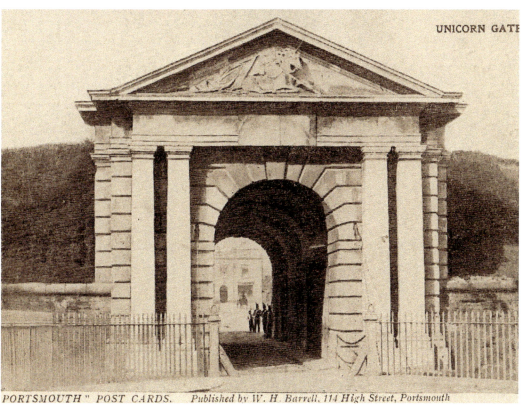

Unicorn Gate, in its original position at the northern end of York Place, beside Anglesea Barracks, c. 1900. As the town grew, moats were filled in, fortifications were dismantled and the gates were removed to more decorative surroundings.

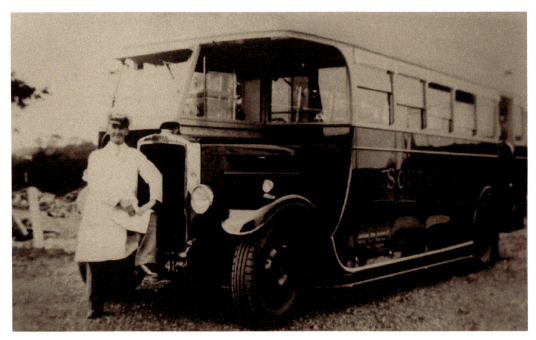

The Southdown bus company was formed in 1915. David Holliday is pictured here with his Leyland – a marque favoured by the company – in Portsmouth, c. 1933. David drove Portsmouth buses for forty years. (Noel Pycroft)

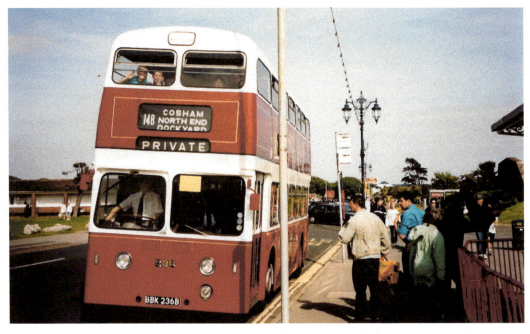

A restored Portsmouth Corporation bus operating nostalgia services at the last ever Portsmouth Bus Rally on Southsea Common, June 2000. The Corporation Transport system started in 1898 with a tram service, replaced by trolleybuses in 1936. Trolleybuses ceased in 1936, and the corporation was privatised by the Tory Thatcher government in 1988.

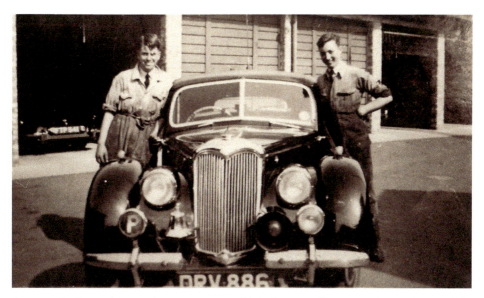

Portsmouth City Police Headquarters was established at Byculla House, former home of the Brickwood's Brewery magnate in Kent Road. The grounds included a cedar tree and a lake replete with goldfish. These cadets are washing and polishing a powerful elegant British-built Riley police car that could outpace anything on the road in 1952. Cars were fuelled from a tank in the grounds. (Tony Hill)

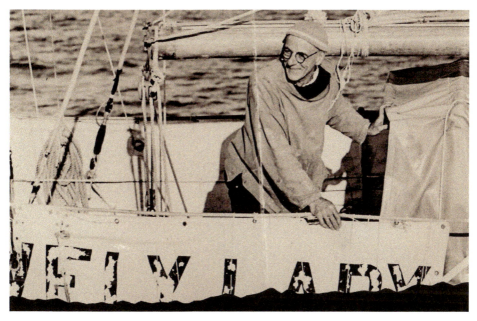

Portsmouth greengrocer Alec Rose, then sixty years old, with his little yacht, a 35-foot cutter built in India named *Lively Lady*, in which he circumnavigated the globe, 28,500 miles, in 1968 – without the use of today's GPS technology. He was a man of great character, nearly drowning off Cape Horn. His rewards included a knighthood and a local Wetherspoons pub named after him. Thanks to local sailor Alan Priddy, there is a plaque on Alec's old shop at No. 38 Osborne Road. (*Portsmouth Evening News*)

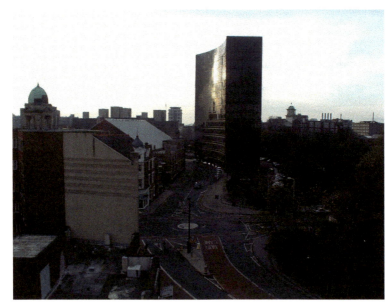

Zurich House, Stanhope Road, dwarfing the old Territorial Army Connaught Hall – famous for its boxing matches – dominates this 1998 view. Today there are fewer open spaces, the one in the foreground next to the black glass tower having been filled by an hotel. Zurich Insurance has moved offices to a business site in Fareham. Their old headquarters has been taken over for residences by an ever-expanding university.

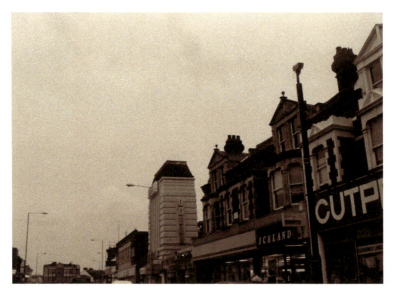

Designed by Andrew Mather, Portsmouth's Odeon, at No. 94 London Road, stands bleak, empty and abandoned. It was closed twelve years ago, in 2008. It was opened on 14 December 1936, with the film *Chick* starring Sydney Howard. It was state of the art, with 1,224 seats in stalls and 600 on the balcony. A new multiplex cinema at Gunwharf Quays has stolen all the shows. When four young men, led by Simon Maitland, entered the derelict site, which had been earmarked for flats, they discovered abandoned lengths of film and equipment, including part of an old film reel from *I Am Legend*, the 2007 movie starring Will Smith, which was set in a world almost devoid of people.

3
Naval Gazing

Portsmouth's naval history and importance was brought into the public eye when Henry VIII's flagship *Mary Rose* was raised in 1982. Old fortifications, much rebuilt, survive as visual reminders of the Royal Navy's Tudor heritage. Two-thirds of a much-reduced fleet is based in Portsmouth.

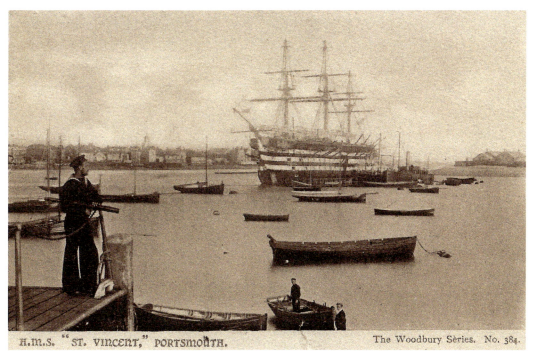

HMS *St Vincent* and Portsmouth Harbour viewed from Gosport in 1905, the last year of *St Vincent*'s service as a training ship for boys. This began in 1862, after a varied service that included transporting French troops to the Baltic. There were two others in her class, with three sliding keels: when these were raised, her draught was less than 6 feet. Decommissioned in 1906, she was broken up at Falmouth. Naval warfare had become more technical and complicated, so specialised training schools were needed.

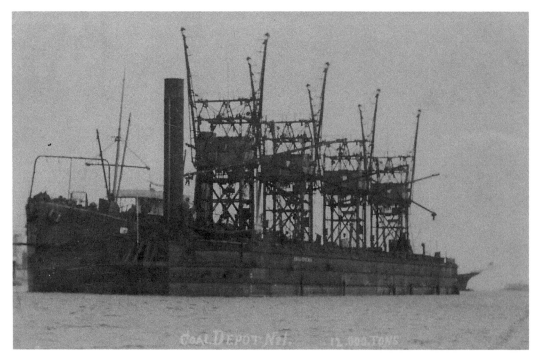

Portsmouth Coal Depot No. 1, *c.* 1914. The steam battleship Dreadnought class hungered for coal, carrying 2,868 long tons (2,914 tons) and an additional 1,120 long tons (1,140 tons) of fuel oil to be sprayed on the coal to increase its burn rate. A young sailor wrote on the back of this card: 'Times be lively this week and we be well looked after, the men are sleeping beside the guns, all vessels are examined as they come up to the harbour and a sharp lookout is kept for the enemy.'

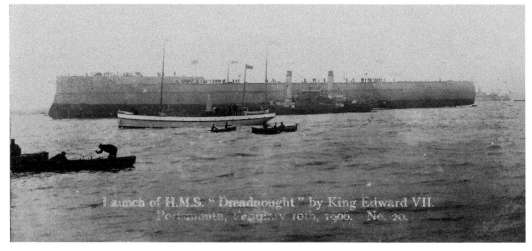

The launch of HMS *Dreadnought*, 10 February 1906. Just one Dreadnought class could have sunk every ship at Trafalgar without hindrance, such had the world changed – the age of Nelson's sailing warships was lost forever. King George VII launched the vessel, while his first cousin Kaiser Wilhelm II led the charge for dreadnoughts of his own. Anglo-German naval rivalry over trade and empire was at its height. In 1907, the new destroyer wireless radio was introduced, allowing the sending and receiving of messages. However, semaphore messaging still played a role.

This is one of two postcards commemorating the tale of Lieutenant Collard and the stokers who refused to get on their knees during a gunnery exercise at the Royal Naval Barracks. Stoker Moody, the alleged ringleader, was given a court martial, prompting a further uprising and an attack on officers' quarters. Flogging sailors continued through the 1930s. Naval medic Mike Hitchman recalled being in Portsmouth's Victorian Detention Quarters in the 1970s, with bread and water rations, drill and marching. Punishment was still harsh.

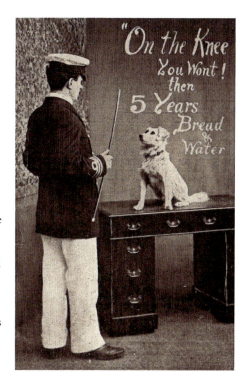

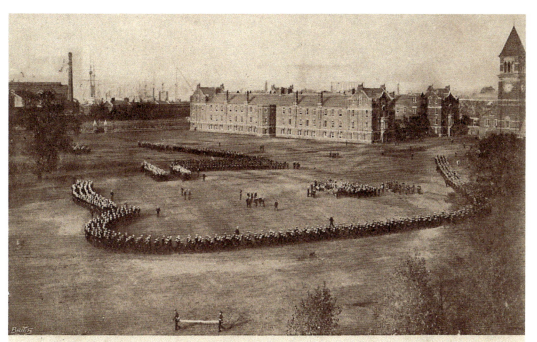

Naval Barracks, c. 1904. Sailors knew how to march. This view looks across the parade ground towards the Dockyard, repairing basins and the old gasworks on the horizon. The old gateway is also in view.

21

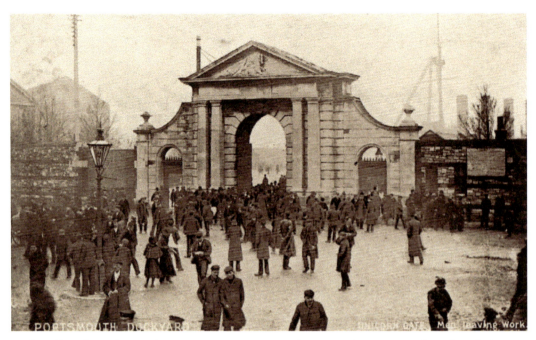

Looking like subjects from an L. S. Lowry painting, men are leaving work at Portsmouth Dockyard, via Unicorn Gate, on to Flathouse Road, *c.* 1910.

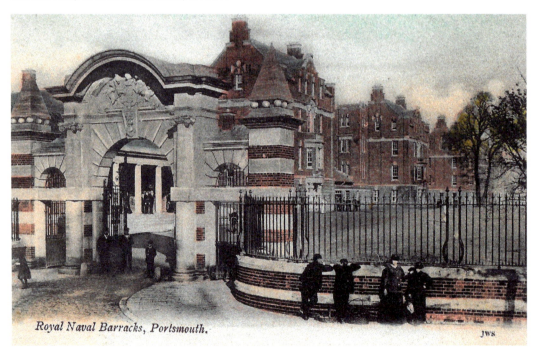

Though a pretty little gate, this is not Lion Gate. Little remains of the old city defences and its ornamental gates. The Lion Gate was removed in 1871. It was re-erected as the gateway to Anglesey Barracks in Queen Street, which later became the Naval Barracks. The gate proved too small and was thus replaced. The old Lion Gate was re-erected as Gateway to the Empire under the Semaphore Tower in 1930.

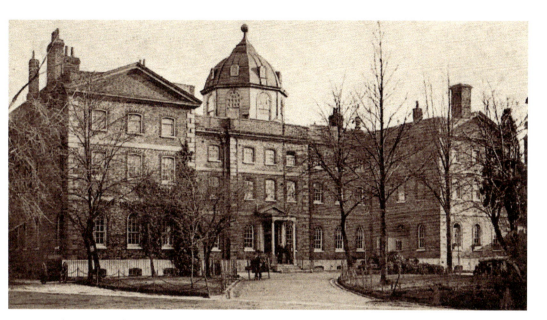

A sedate image of Portsmouth Royal Naval College, 1904. It was created by Queen Mary II in 1694. This grand building was originally the old Royal Naval Hospital for Seamen, becoming the Naval College in 1873. It became renowned across Europe. Chinese graduates of this college are credited with building much of China's twentieth-century navy. Women students were allowed in 1939. The college was closed because of 1983 defence cuts.

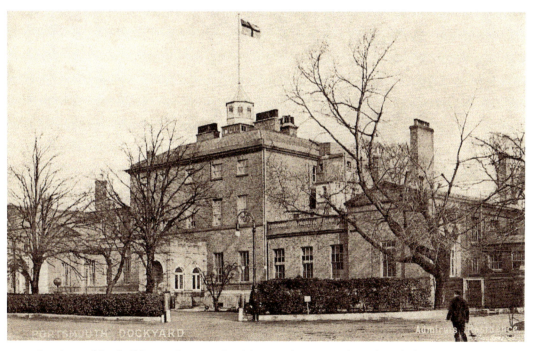

Another striking building in the grounds of the Royal Portsmouth Dockyard, the Admiral's Residence, c. 1904, in the days when Portsmouth had considerable autonomy. The grounds are in good trim, the trees are bare, it looks rather cold and breezy with the flag flying, but all is well.

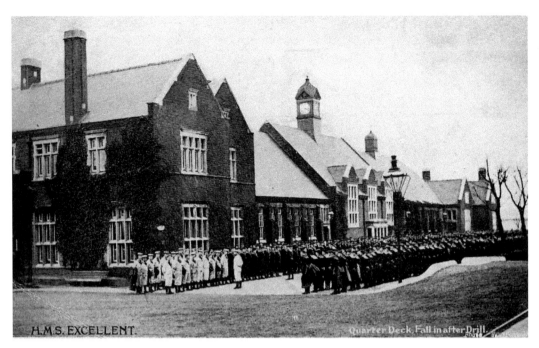

HMS *Excellent*, as the name implies, had the highest standards and extreme discipline. Here sailors fall in after drill, *c*. 1904. The establishment was initially created to train men in gunnery and test new weapons in 1830, then formally established in 1869, and moved to Whale Island in 1869. It ceased to be a separate command in 1985.

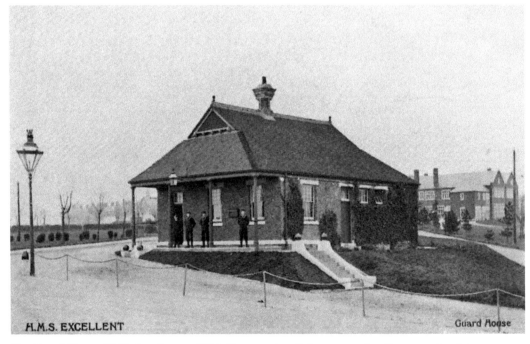

The Guard House, HMS *Excellent*, *c*. 1904. The age of gaslight was waning, Portsmouth gaining an order to generate electricity in 1894. Here, four sailors dutifully pose for the camera.

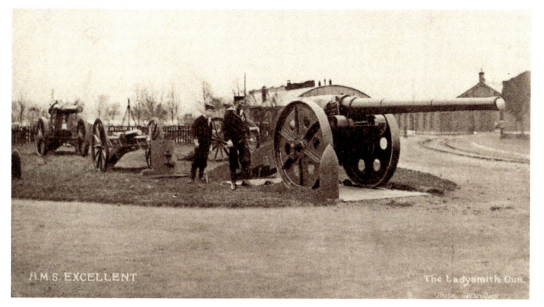

The Ladysmith Gun commemorated the Royal Navy's role in the relief of Ladysmith during the Boer War in 1900, when guns from HMS *Powerful* were hauled to Ladysmith by the ships. This event led to the field gun competition, in which Portsmouth brewers Brickwood's sponsored a trophy, just after the institution of the Inter-Port competition in 1907. It was considered good for drill and naval discipline, and was a Royal Tournament favourite until 1999.

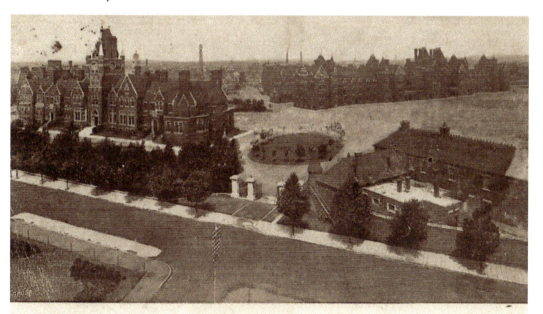

Victoria and Clarence Barracks, Southsea, looking immaculate. Bricks were abundant, produced locally. Lots of chimneys remind us of coal's widespread importance, and there is a large parade ground for marching. Portsmouth City Museum moved from the High Street into part of the old Clarence Barracks. The rest of the area was redeveloped for residential use and a Holiday Inn.

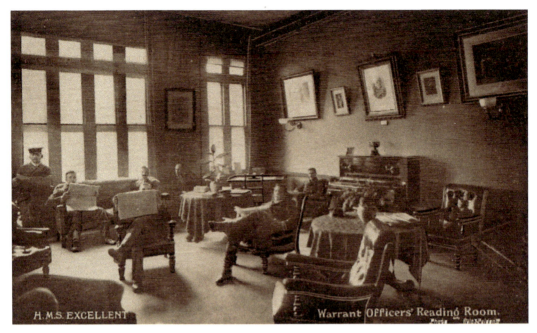

Warrant Officers' spacious Reading Rooms, HMS *Excellent*, c. 1905. In those days, an NCO came from the ranks, a cut above the rest but not quite officer class. Here all looks rather genteel, men relaxing with their broadsheet newspapers in comfortable chairs. There are potted plants, pictures and even a piano. The scene has all the atmosphere of a gentleman's club, with a great empire dependent on the Royal Navy and well-informed leaders at all levels.

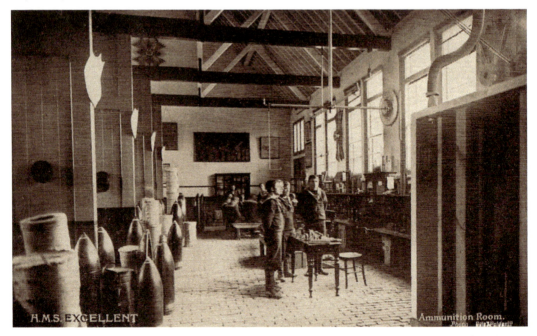

The ammunition room at HMS *Excellent*, c. 1905. This scene marks a fast-changing world. Admiral Sir George Cockburn described the school's purpose as establishing and carrying into effect a system of gunnery 'for the instruction and information of the naval service in that branch of their duty'.

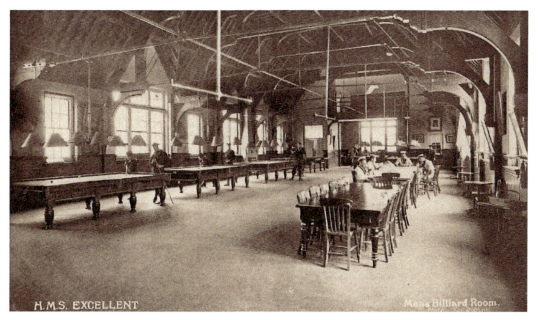

HMS *Excellent* was state of the art and lacked for nothing. This is the billiard room, with well-lit tables. The press gang days were long gone; sailors needed more than harsh discipline.

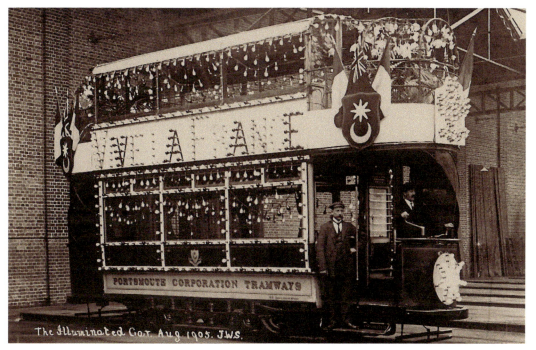

A Portsmouth Corporation tramcar at the long-lost North End Depot, decorated and illuminated for the Entente Cordiale celebrations in 1905. The idea was to end rivalry in the face of the growing power of thirty-five-year-old Germany and naval rivalry. The borough's insignia hangs from the upper deck, a symbol still used today but dating from the twelfth century when Richard I, the great crusader, granted Portsmouth's first charter.

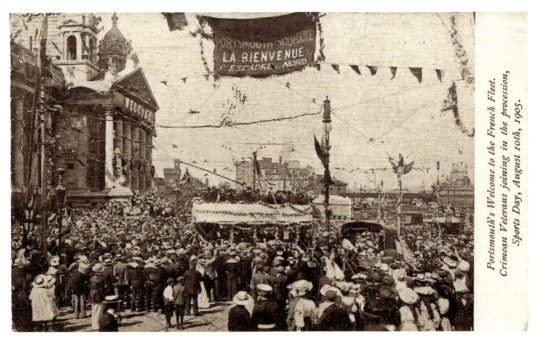

Portsmouth's Welcome to the French Fleet. Crimean Veterans joining in the procession, Sports Day, August 10th, 1905.

Another image celebrating the Entente Cordiale. War with Germany over trade and empire was already on the cards. The Entente was, therefore, very comforting. Here, Crimean War veterans join in the celebrations on Sports Day, 10 August 1905. World war was eleven years away. The arms race was on.

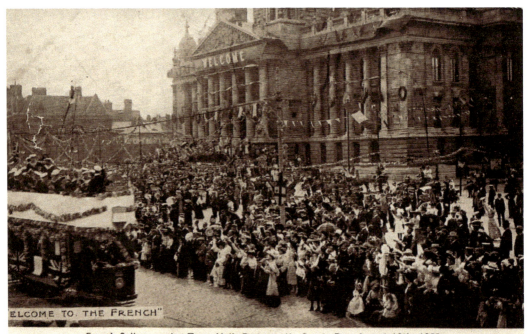

French Sailors passing Town Hall, Portsmouth, Sports Day, August 10th, 1905.

As we can see, the wider population turned out in force to welcome French sailors to a very different and long-lost Portsmouth, 10 August 1905.

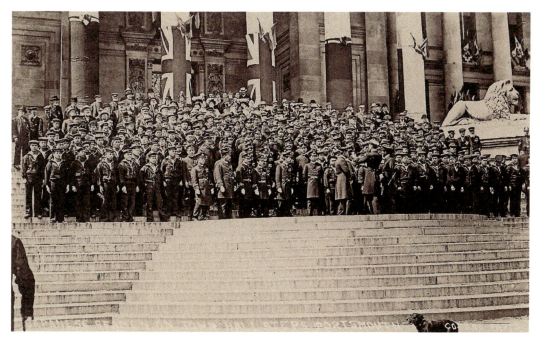

Historically, there have been long ties and cultural exchange between Britain and Japan. Back at the start of the nineteenth century, there was strength and safety in numbers. Here we have visiting Japanese sailors in 1906, massed on the Guildhall steps. Two armed camps were being established.

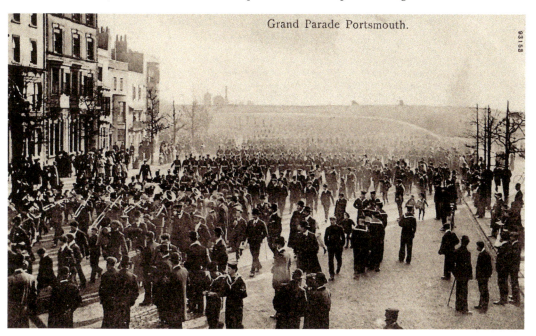

The young sailor who was writing home to his mother in 1905 wrote on this postcard: 'This PC shows our square, and every Sunday we turn out. Things have changed in the last 5 years.' This scene is different today: old Portsmouth has seen major residential development after two world wars. Sailors no longer go on church parade to what is left of nearby Garrison Church.

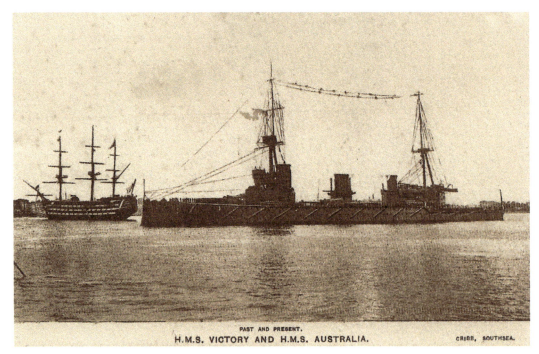

Symbols of change. HMAS *Australia* and HMS *Victory*, Portsmouth Harbour, *c.* 1905. The firepower and defences of these new steam battlecruiser warships could have wiped out an entire fleet at Trafalgar.

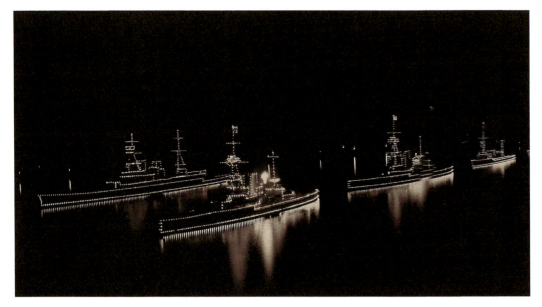

Lieutenant Commander Thomas Woodrooffe made a name for himself at Portsmouth on 20 May 1937, at the Coronation Fleet Review. He was broadcasting live for the BBC Home Service. Radio had come a long way by this time. The lieutenant began, 'At the present moment the whole fleet is lit up. When I say lit up, I mean lit up. Lit up by lots of little fairy lights. The battleships are all lit up, in the shape of a battleship.' When the lights went out, he sounded alarmed, booming, 'The lights have all gone out. The whole fleet has gone. It's not there. It's disappeared.' He rambled on drunkenly for four minutes.

4
Heaven and Hell

German air raids destroyed or badly damaged one-fifth of properties, killing 930 civilians and injuring 2,837. Victoria Park has many memorials to those killed in far-away Imperial wars. Britain's leaders learned nothing from drifting into war in 1914. Economist John Maynard Keynes wrote two relevant books: *The Economic Consequences of the Peace* and *The Economic Consequences of Mr Churchill*. He was ignored.

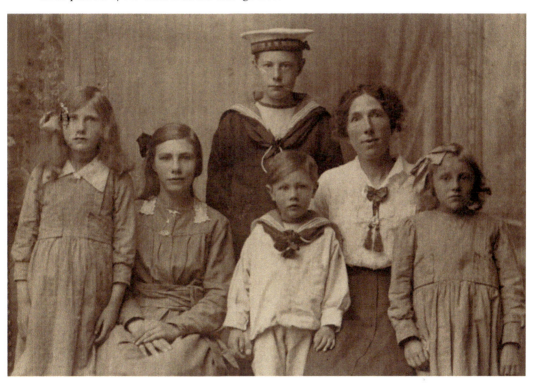

This Portsmouth family photograph shows an anxious and worn-out mother – old before her time. There is no father present, the eldest boy is being prepared for a naval life in the run-up to the First World War, and the eldest girl appears serene while the others show tension and maybe fear.

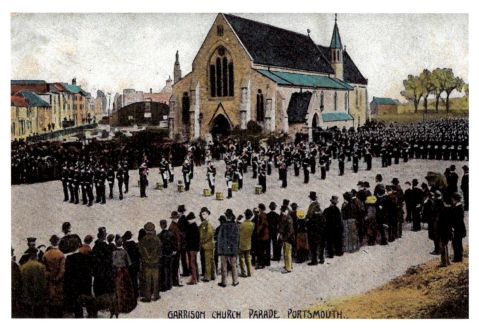

Royal Garrison Church Parade, 1905. Domus Dei was a hospital and almshouse built on this site. King Henry VIII stole it from the Church, and consequently, the poor suffered more. The building was initially used as an armoury; then a mansion was built, becoming home for the military governor. Charles II married Catherine of Braganza in the chapel. Only the ruins of the church survived a bombing raid in 1941. All traces of medieval buildings were lost.

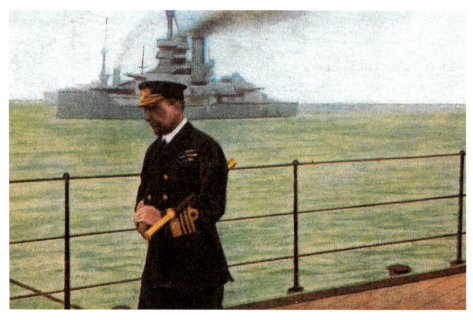

Admiral Sir David Beaty, aboard the *Iron Duke*, which was the lead ship of the Dreadnought class. Built in Portsmouth Dockyard and launched ten months later, she became Beaty's Grand Fleet flagship, with massive guns and a top speed of 24.5 mph. Ending her days as an anti-aircraft platform during the Second World War, she was broken up for scrap in the late 1940s.

Right: High Street, Old Portsmouth. St Thomas's Tower is prominent. When Portsmouth became a city, St Thomas's was chosen to be a cathedral to enhance its prospects. The buildings and little shops seen here were demolished, making way for Cathedral Green. (*Portsmouth News*)

Below: The First World War accelerated aircraft development. The interwar years inspired a spirit of adventure, none more adventurous than this former secretary turned flyer and record-breaker Amy Johnson, who is seen here addressing the crowd at Fratton Park football ground on 4 September 1930. Amy mysteriously lost her life when she was serving as an RAF ferry pilot, ditching over the Thames Estuary. (*Portsmouth News*)

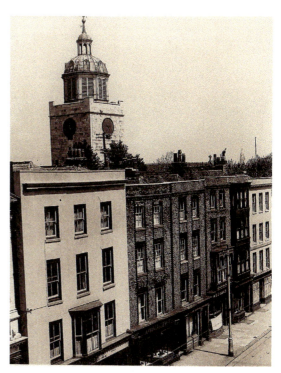

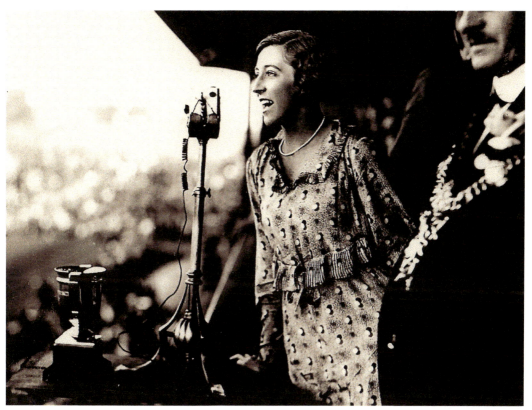

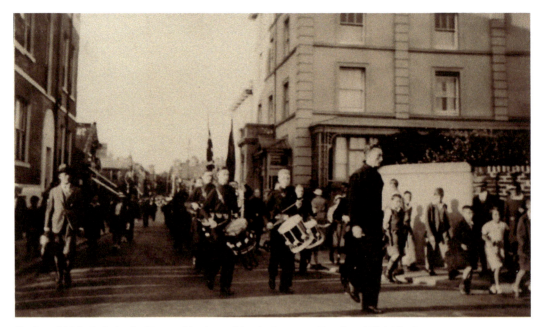

Sir Oswald Mosley's fascist 'Brownshirts' marching in Burgoyne Road, *c.* 1926. The interwar years saw the proud German people unfairly punished for starting the First World War. Worldwide, the wealthy cut back and unemployment exploded. In Europe, the working classes turned to fascism for hope and escape. Poorly educated and starving, even Britain veered towards Nazism. Hitler was a deranged the First World War veteran who led the charge, and another world war was inevitable.

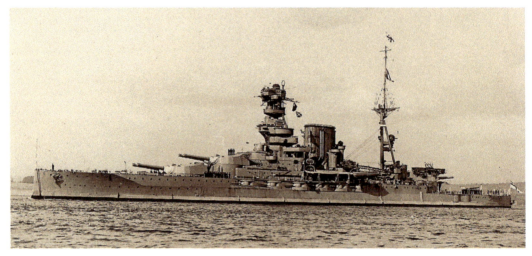

HMS *Barnham* in the Solent, March 1924. Like other British battleships, *Barnham* suffered the weakness of inadequate deck armour. It wasn't just aircraft that had advanced; so had weapons. Churchill, in charge of the Navy, resisted deck armour, sealing the fate of this ship, along with *Hood*, *Repulse* and *The Prince of Wales*. *Barnham* sank within four minutes of being hit, after its magazines exploded – 855 sailors perished. George Elliot had been working as a railway engine cleaner at Fratton when he was called up into the Navy and posted to *HMS Barnham*, a Queen Elizabeth class battleship. He was lucky to survive its sinking. A Portsmouth woman was convicted and jailed for witchcraft because she predicted the sinking of *HMS Hood* at a seance.

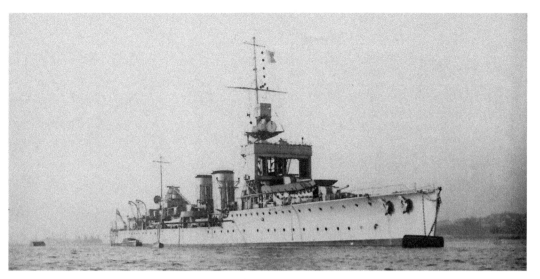

HMS *Glamorgan* was another Portsmouth-based ship – although with a name symbolic of Wales. It was laid down in Glasgow on 24 January 1917 and launched on 29 December the same year. The ship saw varied action until hit by a manned torpedo on 8 July 1944. Heavily damaged, with thirty-seven lives lost though still afloat, *Dragon* had a final purpose to serve. It was towed to the mock breakwater near Courseulles, then scuttled, on 20 July, to become part of the artificial Mulberry Harbour.

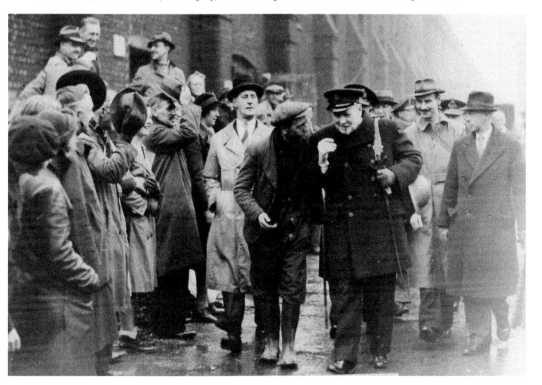

A dockyard worker asks then plain Winston Churchill for his cigar stub in 1941. He may have been a half-English aristocrat, but his American mother gave him traits perfectly suited to working an audience. (*Portsmouth News*)

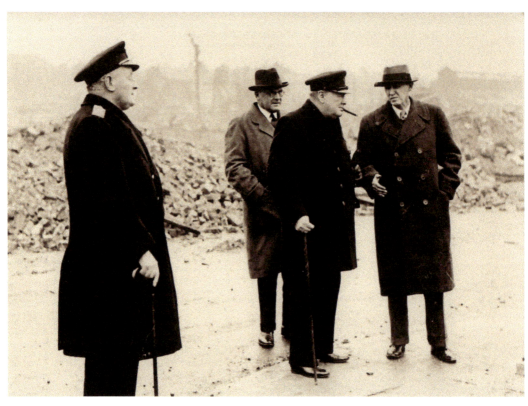

Above: Surveying damage to Old Portsmouth, 1941. Left to right: Admiral Sir William James, Regional Commissioner Harold Butler, Prime Minister Churchill, and the American President's representative Harry Hopkins. (*Portsmouth News*)

Left: Mabel Fucher on a bicycle, with sister Alice, outside Margate Road air-raid shelter. 'I worked in an office at John Dyers shop. They sold everything, clothes, furnishings, until the big blitz. There were two raids on 10 January 1941. They rescued a lot but the Germans came back and finished it off. I lost my job. You often heard of people being killed overnight. The labour office sent me to work at Fire Brigade HQ.' (Mabel Warren)

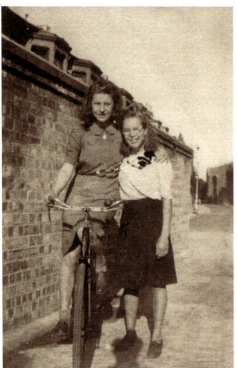

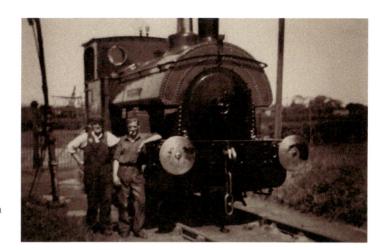

A gasworks saddle tank locomotive at Hilsea with Jim Evans, left, in early wartime. (Dave Brunnen)

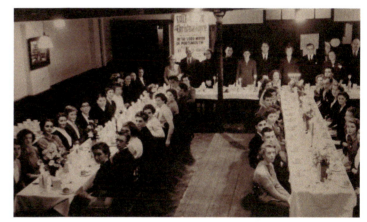

The Salvation Army 'torchbearers' at The Mission, Albert Road. (John Mason)

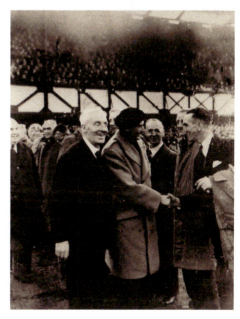

Portsmouth City football player Bill Moffat shakes hands with Field Marshal Lord Montgomery. (John Mason)

5
Seaside

Southsea's Tudor castle took only six months to build. The country had many enemies after Henry VIII abolished the Roman Catholic Church in 1536. Fortifications and guns were the order of the day. Relics of that age remain, but since the nineteenth century, the marshy common land has been well drained. Grand monuments to the Victorian developer Thomas Ellis Owen – who built St Jude's Church to encourage the wealthy to buy his large villas – survived Second World War bombing, though the sedate world of fine ladies on the promenade, bathing machines for ladies' modesty and the more gaudy entertainments of the 1950s, 1960s and 1970s are long lost.

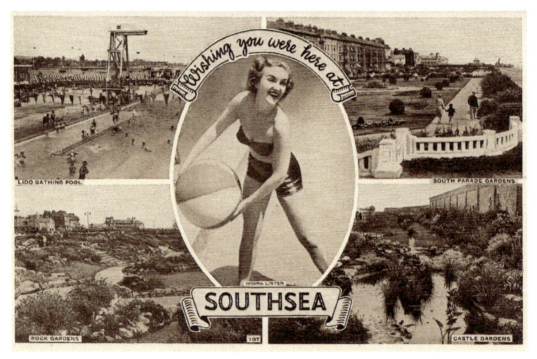

This 1950s postcard says it all about the innocence and simple pleasures of a holiday in Southsea. The young woman's outfit is about as racy as life got for common people!

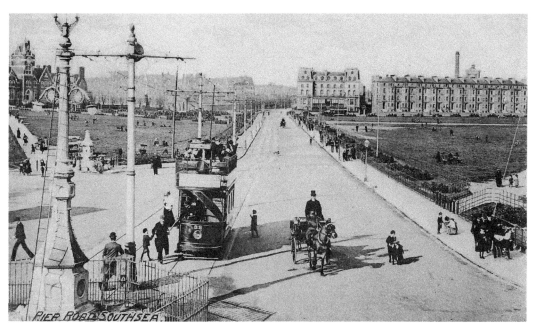

Pier Road, Southsea, *c.* 1908. Trees are bare in this wintry scene, very much evoking a Sunday afternoon promenade, the people dressed for cold weather. Corporation trams were kept busy all year, en route to the pier and seafront. Originally, trams were intended to transfer passengers from the town railway station to the Isle of Wight ferries. Portsmouth Corporation Transport was formed by Act of Parliament in 1898, privatised by Thatcher's government in 1988. In the distance, we can also see the long-gone Victoria and Clarence Barracks on the other side of Pembroke Gardens. The Duke of Clarence visited Portsmouth in 1827, to present colours to the Royal Marines light infantry, leading to an association that lives on.

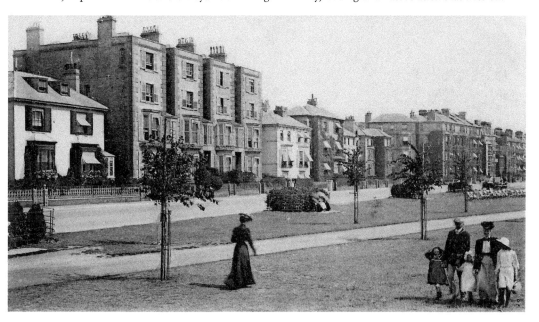

A very early Edwardian scene, with a well-dressed lady walking out in her finery along Clarence Esplanade on a summer's day. These were the days when women needed chaperones to walk out with men.

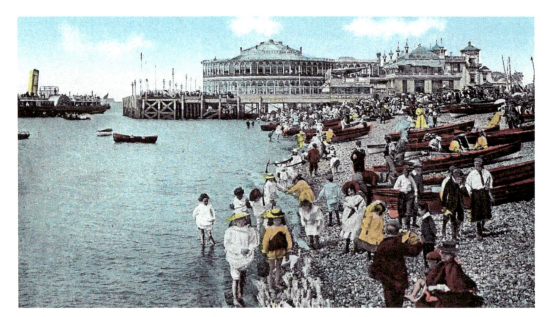

This happy summer scene of *c.* 1910 is dominated by Clarence Pier, built in 1861 and opened by the Prince and Princess of Wales. The pier's popularity increased when the tramway was extended here in 1886. The length of the pier had been increased in 1905 and again in 1932, offering all a modern holidaymaker could need. Here we see an Isle of Wight paddle steamer making off to Queen Victoria's favourite island. Sadly, this curious pier structure was destroyed by a German raid on 1 June 1941. The pier was rebuilt more modestly and opened again in 1961.

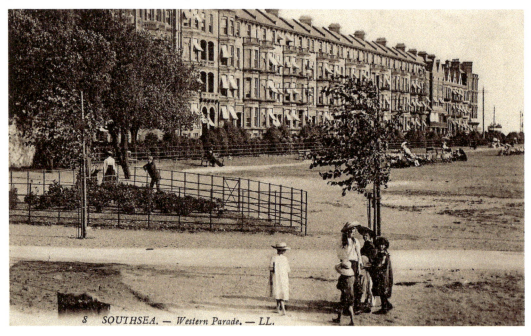

Western Parade, Southsea, *c.* 1908, with happy children relaxing in a park-like world of parasols, summer and heat. Who really needed the war that was on the way, the war for which the local dockyard was then building dreadnoughts?

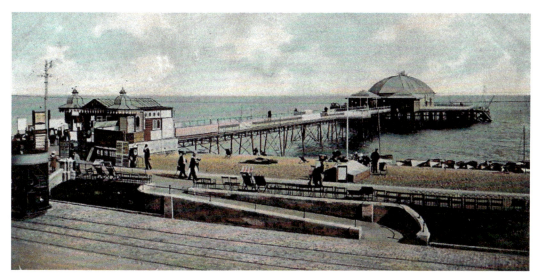

Opened by Prince Edward of Saxe-Coburg in 1879, 400 yards long and supposedly fireproof, this is South Parade Pier in 1904, just before the blaze that destroyed it later that year. It was opened in 1879 to cash in on the Isle of Wight steamer traffic. A rail branch was built from Fratton Station with a terminus near the pier, opening in 1885. It was little used, and the tracks were lifted in 1926, twelve years after closure. The precious land was used for housing, but the line's curve can be traced along Goldsmith Avenue.

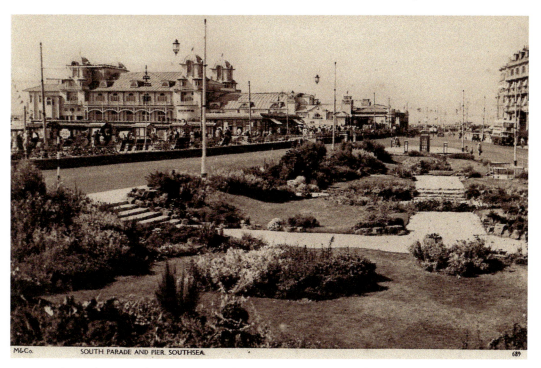

South Parade Pier, mid-1930s. Apparently Henry VIII watched his flagship *Mary Rose* sink from this point in 1545. The pier was bought by the corporation after the 1904 fire, rebuilt at a cost of £85,000, then burned down twice more, most famously during the filming of the rock opera *Tommy* in 1974. All around this scene are well-kept gardens, indicating it was a thriving age for seaside holidays and day trips.

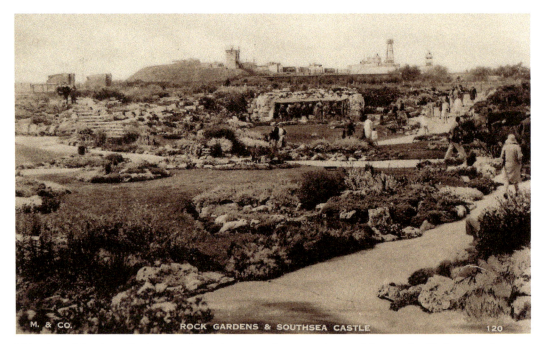

This view of Southsea Castle, over the rock gardens, has seen changes. Most noticeable here are the strict dress and decorum of those enjoying themselves in this mid-1930s image. The seaside is not what it used to be, but Southsea is still popular for those who want to promenade and jog. The garden area has been reformed for practicalities and safety.

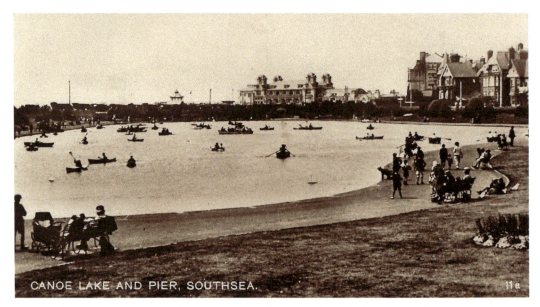

Canoe Lake, *c.* 1907. This was built on an old rubbish tip, to help with drainage problems. Again, the image shows that a way of life has been lost, though the lake is still there. It was the work of Borough Engineer Boulnois, in an area originally named The People's Park and prior to that The Great Morass. It provided a popular spot for relaxation and safe boating. South Parade Pier is prominent, but the last rebuild did not include a theatre. The pier shows were once a big seaside attraction.

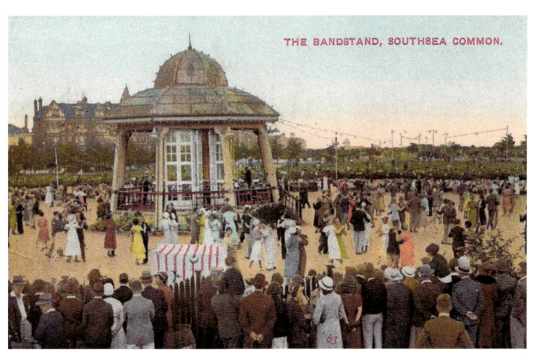

The bandstand, c. 1936. How beautiful this scene is, suggesting a world of love and peace, elegance and style. The site is now a skateboard park.

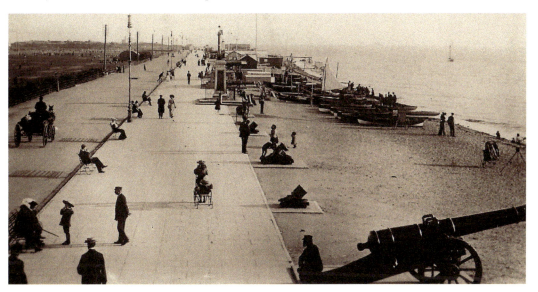

The telegraph poles and electric light informs us that this image shows a modern age in 1908. Female modesty and old-fashioned social distancing look quaint and lonely. A big cannon on display reminds us that Portsmouth has had much to do with war and empire. A gun like this used to be fired every evening. A sense of peace is enhanced by the clip-clopping horse-drawn carriage. There are no cars in sight, though the common, used by the military even after it was sold to the corporation, looks very busy. In August 1782, Scot David Tyrie, a dockyard civil servant, was hanged for twenty-three minutes, beheaded and quartered for selling information to the French.

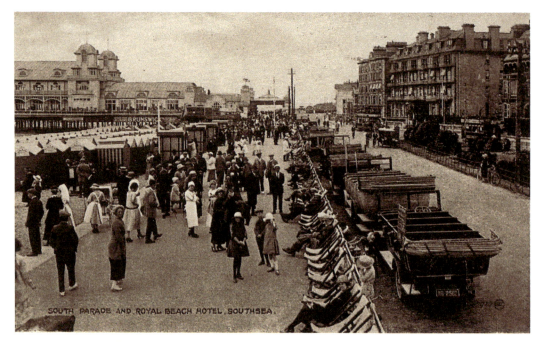

The 'Roaring Twenties' have arrived, the 'Great War' is over, major trade depression is still a few years away. So it is time for a charabanc trip to the seaside and all the wonders of South Parade Pier. Ladies' fashions are less restrictive, but hats are still the order of the day. Across the road, old open-top trams are still in service.

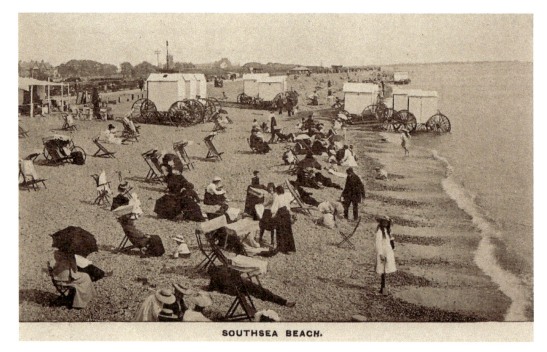

Southsea Beach, c. 1909. Eastney Royal Marine barracks is on the horizon, now long gone. Female modesty is a must, so the bathing machines are out in force.

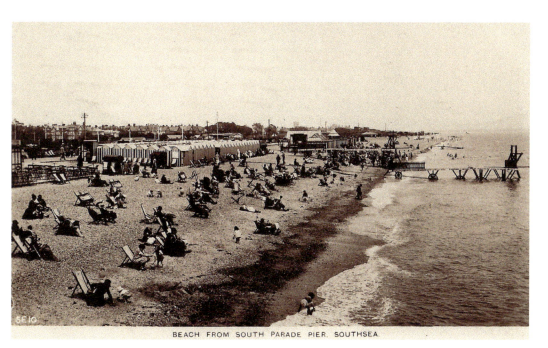

The same scene, *c.* 1920. Bathing machines have been replaced by marquees, with the dress code and bathers looking more relaxed.

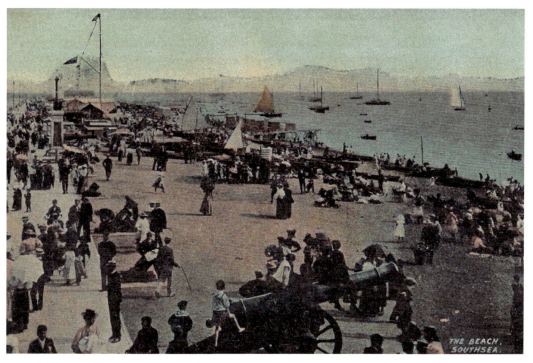

A bright and breezy scene. Lots of little boats are out on the water; people in rather serious dress belie the fact this is summer 1908. The field gun may be dated, which is why it is ornamental, but it is getting much interest from imaginative little boys.

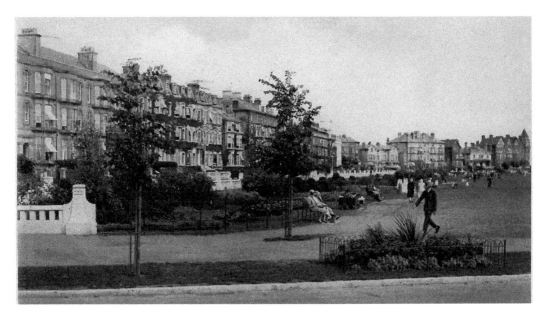

Southsea came back to life in the 1920s after the sea change of the First World War. Ladies' dresses were shorter, and confidence greater. These large houses close to the seafront were ideal for the plethora of holidaymakers.

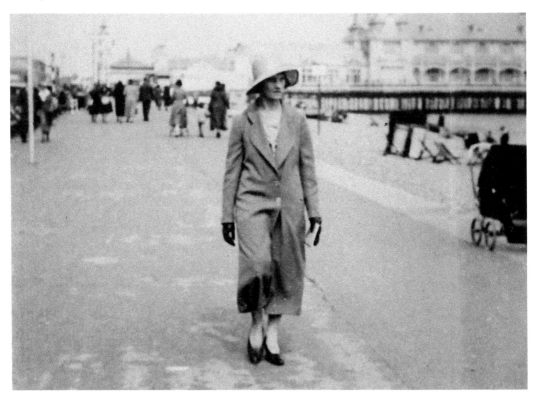

Mrs Mason walking past South Parade Pier, 1920s. Ladies never went out hatless. Her expression is circumspect. (John Mason)

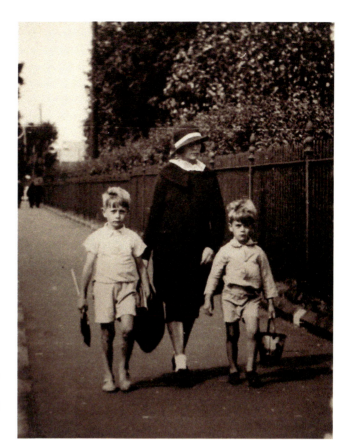

A more relaxed Mrs Mason on her way, with two small sons, to Southsea beach in the 1930s – fulfilling the traditional mother's role, a role that has much changed since the 1950s.

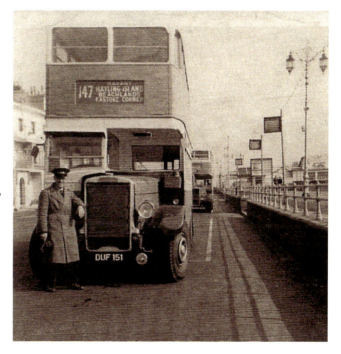

A Southdown *Leyland* double-decker from pre-war days, near South Parade Pier. Founded in 1915 by Alfred Douglas Mackenzie and Alfred Cannon, Southdown was absorbed into the National Bus Company and then sold off following 1988's deregulation, the name disappearing. In its heyday, Southdown ran luxury tours at home and abroad.

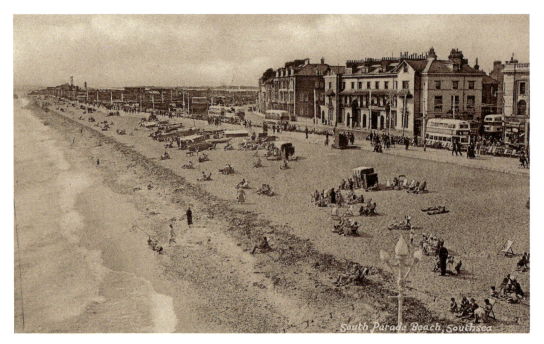

Looking over South Parade Beach, 1949. The city is getting back to normal. The beach isn't crowded but there is an atmosphere of relaxation. Trolleybuses have replaced trams, but will be gone within the next twenty years.

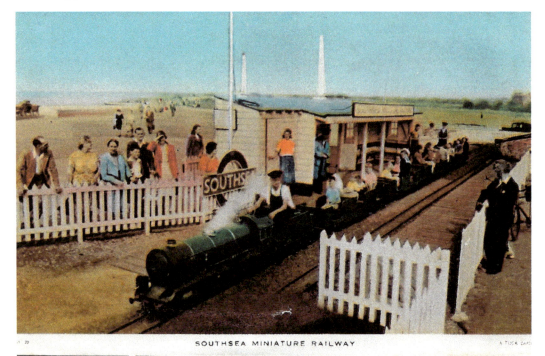

Southsea miniature railway, 1950s, when it was a popular attraction. But steam railways were fading away, as was the taste for simple seaside pleasures.

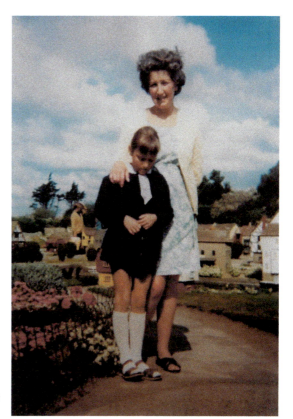

Right: Southsea model village has moved with the times. This 1960s image speaks of a brief age of hope and innocence. (Shirley Warne)

Below: Sailor Ivan Warne out with his family, looking rather warm, 1960s. The summers in our mind seemed so much nicer then. (Shirley Warne)

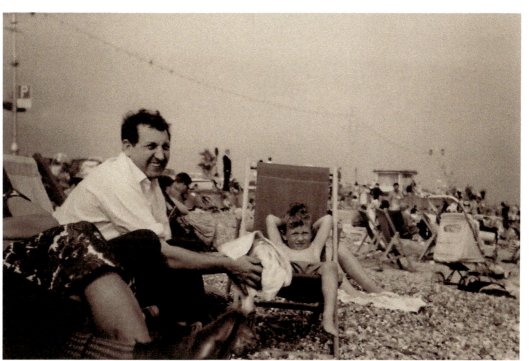

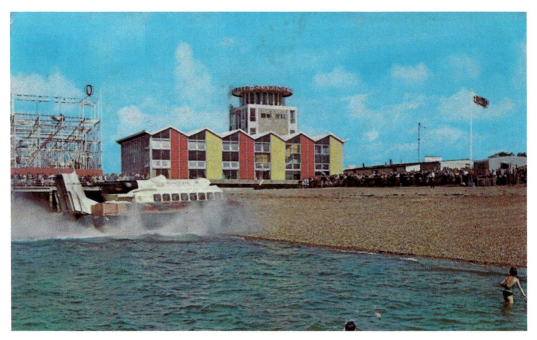

People used to gaze in wonder at the new hovercraft service to the Isle of Wight, where the craft were built originally by Sir Christopher Cockerell in a hangar at Cowes. This scene marks the opening of the new Clarence Pier, which was destroyed by bombs because of its strategic importance.

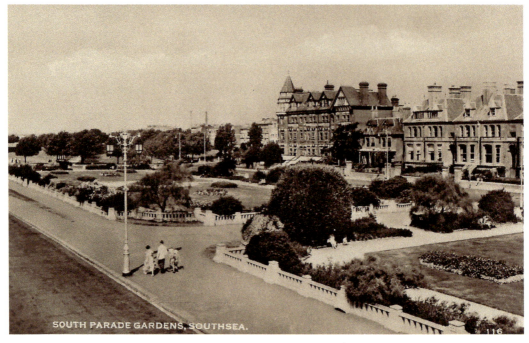

A dream scene from the 1950s. A little English family is having fun in South Parade Gardens before the age of 'sunny Spain'. On the back of this postcard is written: 'Having a nice time, thinking of you. We have come to Rhyde for the day. It is a lovely day. Have been on a coach tour.'

6

Tricorn Haze

Portsmouth had a high population density of 200 per acre in 1939. While the bombs were falling in 1941, a council committee was optimistically planning a new and better place, with only seventy people per acre. That would mean moving people north, east and west beyond the city limits, across the water that had defined Portsmouth for centuries. The nation was near bankrupt, but hopes and political promises were abundant.

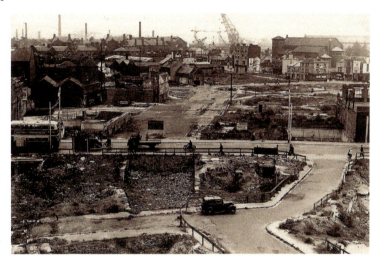

It's amazing how much was left standing in this view of the city centre from the north, looking over Charlotte Street, late 1940s. This is the site that greeted young architect Owen Luder when he met property developer Alec Coleman in the early 1960s. (Portsmouth City Museum)

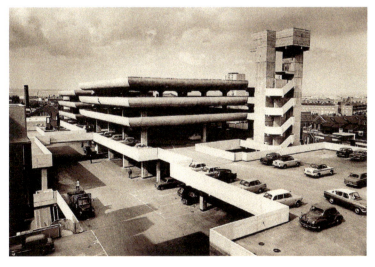

Here was Owen Luder and partner Rodney Gordon's solution to reviving the city centre, shining in the daylight of 1966 when it first opened. It was the Tricorn Centre. (*Portsmouth News*)

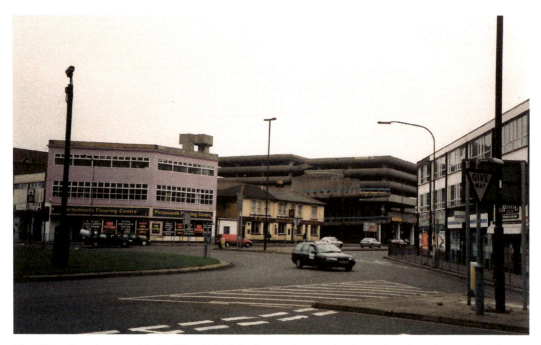

The Tricorn looming over Market Way, 2004. It looks run-down and rather sad, as does the now closed Dorchester Pub next door. Demolition is nigh, marking the end of what was a dream world for some and nightmare for others.

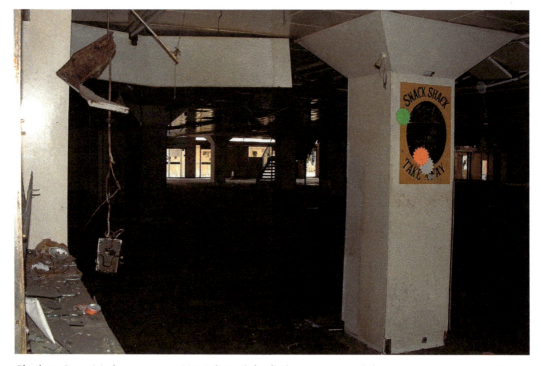

Charlotte Street Market, summer 1997. What is left of it has gone around the corner into Commercial Road. The shops have gone too, along with The Tricorn.

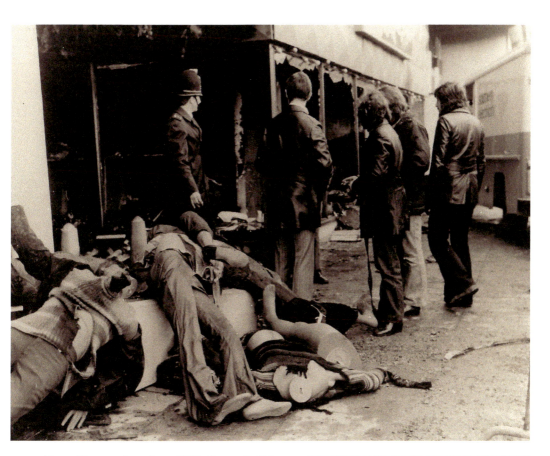

Above: The morning after a 1970s fire at the Tricorn Centre. Local DJ and ultimately the Tricorn Club Manager Pete Cross is far right, and right on with his dress sense. (*Portsmouth News*)

Right: Another sexy 1970s image, with the band Freedom back again at the famous Tricorn Club. (Pete Cross)

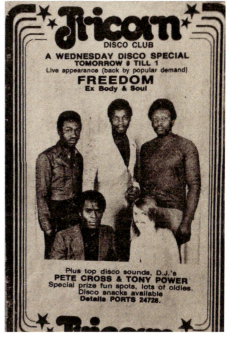

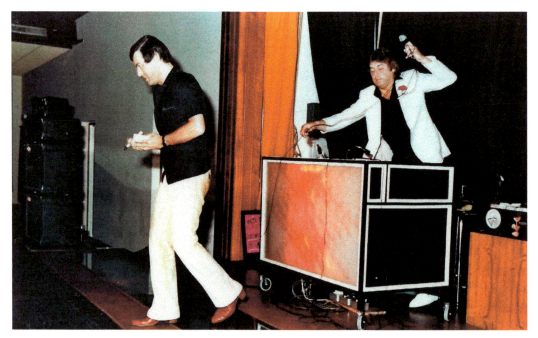

DJs Tony Blackburn and Pete Cross giving their all at the Tricorn Club in the late 1970s. (Pete Cross)

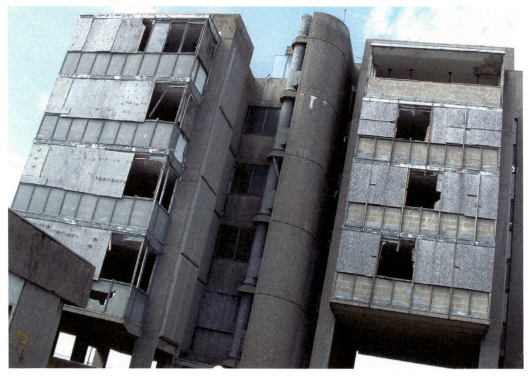

This image of the Tricorn flats speaks volumes about the faded hopes of the 1960s and the concrete future. They were expected to house staff from the neighbouring Royal Portsmouth Hospital, which was turned to dust nearly a decade earlier.

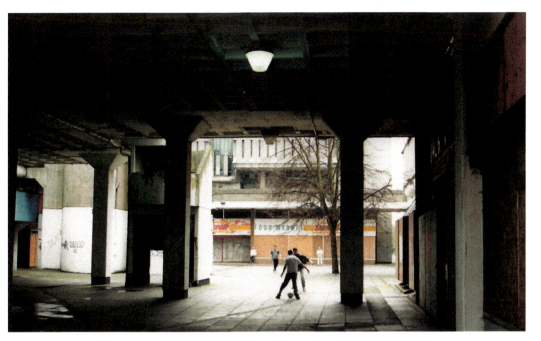

Architect Owen Luder explained his concept for The Tricorn, including how its centre was this square. The tree is still alive in this picture, as are the kids kicking a ball around. The Tricorn Club and its incarnations as Basins and Grannies – with all its different manifestations of transitory youth culture – is derelict.

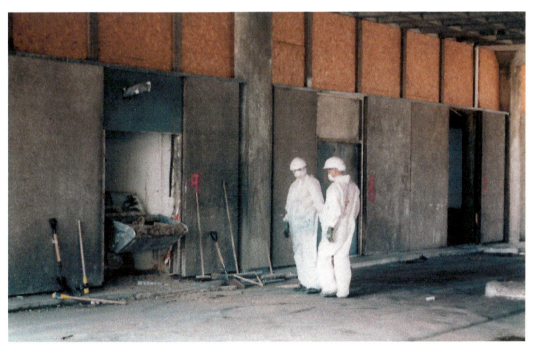

The boarded-up Tricorn complex attracted the island's homeless, hopeless and drug addicts. Pigeons also moved in, which is why these demolition workers are wearing protective clothing to clear out years of their droppings.

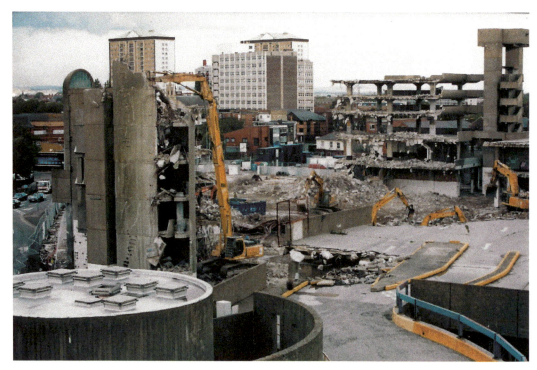

In this Tricorn demolition scene from 2004, it looks as if the Luftwaffe has returned.

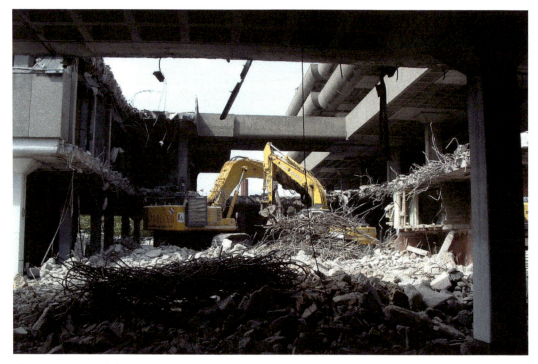

The Tricorn dream did not last. The centre failed for many reasons. Here, one of Controlled Demolition's giant machines is pulverising the concrete, exposing a fortune in recyclable steel.

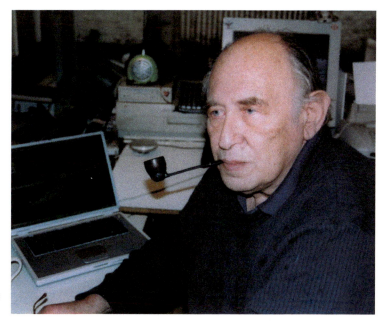

Rodney Gordon during an interview with Robert Cook in London, 2004. He began his career with London County Council designing new flats for the people bombed out by the blitz, before being headhunted by Owen Luder. These two Londoners wanted to create a better living, work and shopping space in the bombed-out northern quarter of the city – the Tricorn Centre.

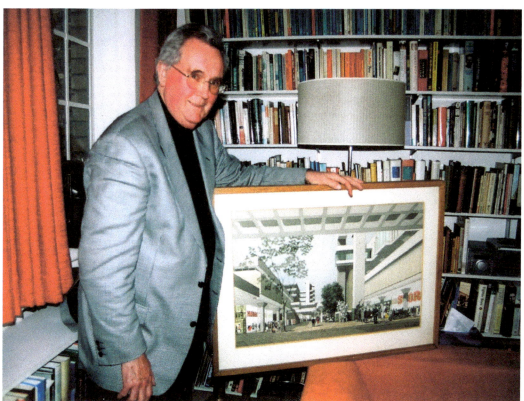

Owen Luder at his London home, with an artist's impression of the new Tricorn Centre. He took developer Alec Coleman's requirement for car parking, a little retail and marketplace into a groundbreaking example of Brutalism, which was symbolic of the nation's hopes and further decline.

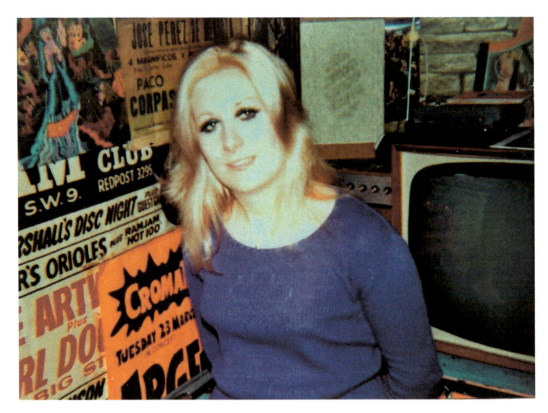

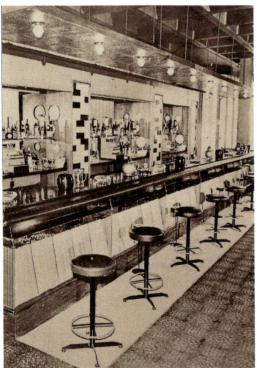

Above: Jan Cross, a girl of her times back in the days when she and husband Pete had so much fun at The Tricorn. Pete said he was a closet trendy, including being a mod on a motor scooter. (For more information, see *The Tricorn: The Life and Death of a Sixties Icon*, by Celia Clark and Robert Cook.)

Left: The Lounge Bar at The Tricorn Club, from the original advertising brochure.
(Pete Cross)

7

In Dock

Portsmouth's Royal Dockyard declined from employing over 24,000 in the early 1950s to 16,500 in the 1960s and fewer than 10,000 in 2020. Many were given redundancy notices just before the Falklands War when Thatcher was hurrying to make cuts. The yard boomed from its early days when Henry VII chose it as the site of a new Royal Dockyard. There was plenty of space allowed for building a new fleet. Wooden warships needed 300 mature oak trees and sawyers to do the hard dirty work in the sawpits. Ships from all over the world visited: best remembered was Russian cruiser *Ordzonikdze* in April 1956. Russia was outraged to discover that MI6 deployed a former naval diver, Commander 'Buster' Crabbe, to spy on the keel. Crabbe's headless body was found in Chichester Harbour fourteen months later.

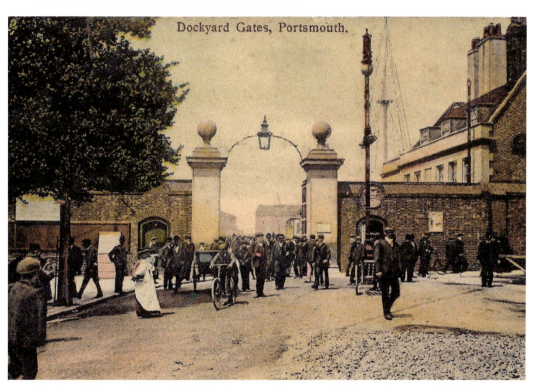

Dockyard 'Victory Gate', *c.* 1907. Bicycles were still an expensive luxury but a worthwhile investment. Well into the 1960s, dockyard end of shift saw the local roads congested by an outburst of cyclists. The Revd Thomas Dolling wrote, in 1896, that there were 10,000 men working here fitting out and repairing ships: 'Beyond the dockyard walls was a world of cockpits, pubs, brothels, seedy back streets, drunken and rootless sailors.'

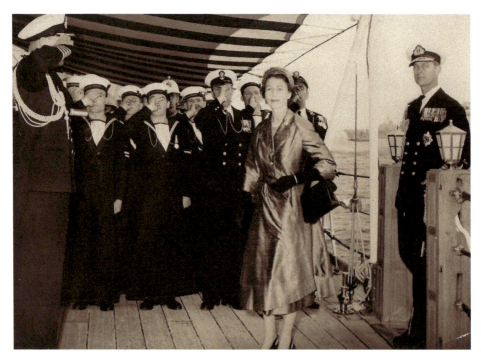

Queen Elizabeth being piped on board HMS *Glasgow* at the 1953 fleet review off Spithead. The Duke of Edinburgh wears the uniform of Admiral of the Fleet. This review by the reigning monarch had been a tradition for over 400 years. (Shirley Warne)

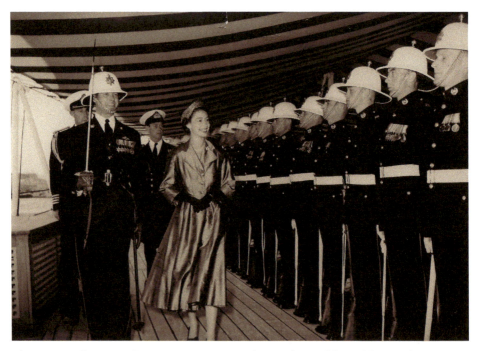

The Queen, still awaiting her coronation, inspects the Royal Guard formed by Royal Marines on her visit to HMS *Glasgow*. (Shirley Warne)

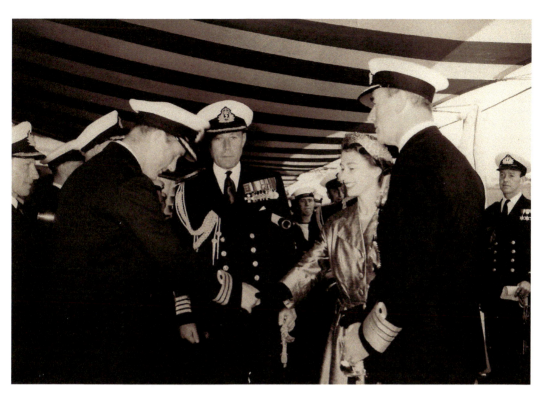

Everybody who was anybody in the Royal Navy was here to greet the new Queen and her illustrious husband, here on HMS *Glasgow* off Spithead, 1953. (Shirley Warne)

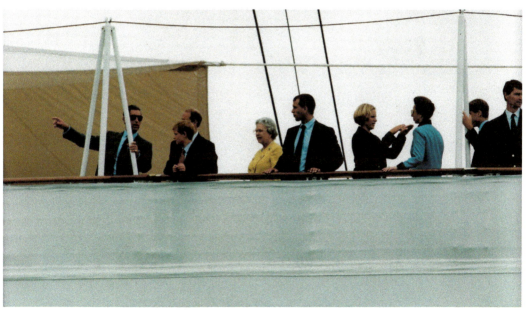

The Queen, accompanied by most of her immediate family except Prince Philip. The vessel is seen here pulling away from the south railway jetty in Portsmouth Harbour, 7 August 1997. The royal family were sailing in troubled times and about to lose their royal yacht. (*Portsmouth News*)

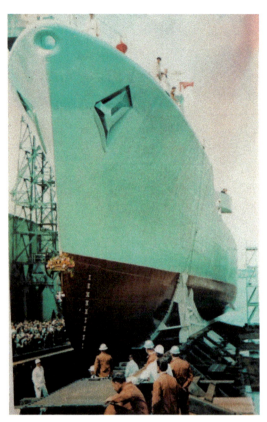

Left: The dockyard has undertaken some challenges, including lengthening HMS *Victorious* by 30 feet. HMS *Andromeda*, a Leander class frigate, was the last warship built here in May 1967. (*Portsmouth News*)

Below: Ice Patrol Ship HMS *Endurance*, July 1999. The late Captain Nick Barker commanded the ship's predecessor of the same name. He was warned to shut up or get out of the service for his warnings about Argentinian build-up before the Falklands War. The dockyard was already being run down as part of massive Thatcher defence cuts. The 4,050-tonne passenger ship was bought from the Norwegians in 1992, being scrapped in 2012.

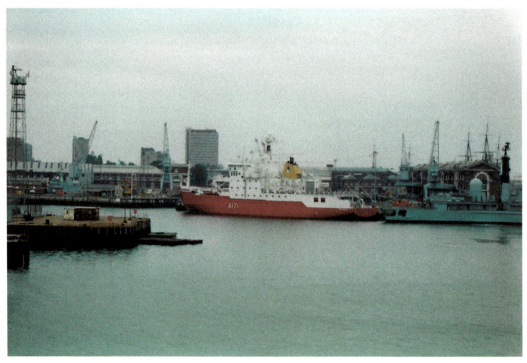

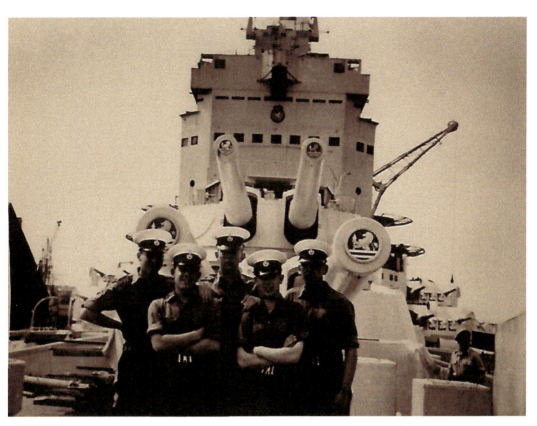

David Rowlands, front left, on board HMS *Protector*, Portsmouth Dockyard, 1957. As a regular Royal Marine, he recalled serving with National Serviceman actor Harry H. Corbett of *Steptoe* fame. David said, 'He was a fine marine, took it seriously.' (David Rowlands)

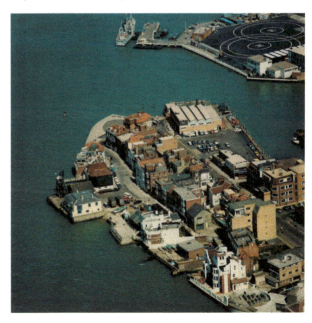

A fine 1960s view of Portsmouth's Point and the helicopter pad of HMS *Vernon*. Richard I established a naval function here, and it became a dock for royal galleys. The name HMS *Vernon* was conferred in 1923. It played a key defence role as an ordnance depot, training mine divers and D-Day troops. Closure came with Thatcher's 1986 defence cuts, the corporation taking over, and the site ultimately became a shopping centre, Gunwharf Quays. (Simmons Aerofilms)

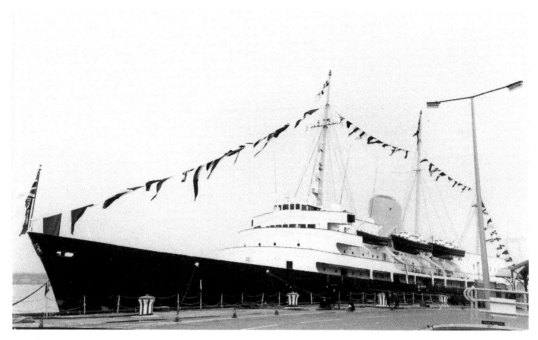

Royal Yacht *Britannia* in Portsmouth Dockyard, August 1997, shortly before the New Labour government scrapped a £50 million refit with new engines. The vessel was decommissioned, signalling a new era for royalty.

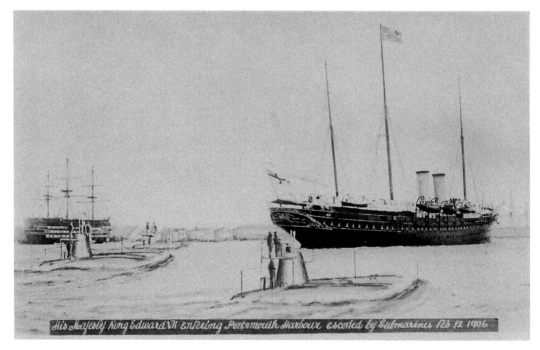

His Majesty King Edward VII, affectionately known as 'Tum Tum' because of his love of nine-course meals, enters Portsmouth Harbour on his yacht, *Albert and Victoria*, escorted by submarines, 1906. This was one of the first ships to be fitted with radio, following Marconi's successful trials off the Isle of Wight.

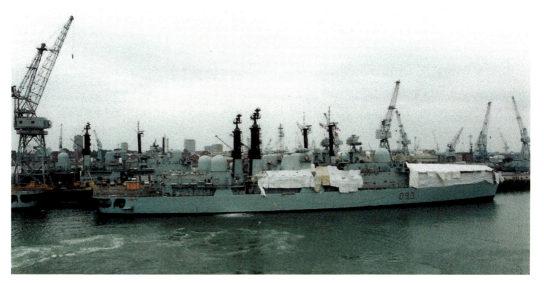

HMS *Southampton* in Portsmouth Harbour, built by Vosper Thornycroft and launched in 1979, was scrapped in Turkey, rather than the local Pounds yard. She was a Type 42 Sheffield class destroyer, pictured here in Portsmouth Dockyard in 1998, a year before being decommissioned.

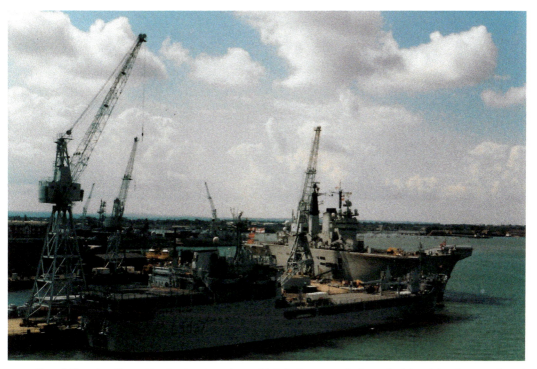

Royal Fleet Auxiliary ship *Sir Geraint*, pictured left in Portsmouth. Launched in 1967, she served until May 2003. Pictured right is the pride of the fleet, flagship *HMS Ark Royal*. Built by San Hunter, she took two and a half years to build and was launched by the Queen Mother in 1981. Five Royal Navy ships have carried this name, dating back to the Spanish Armada. Large crowds watched aircraft carrier *Ark Royal* being towed away bound for Turkey after being decommissioned early following the 2010 defence review.

8
Power and Glory

Where there are politicians there is power; where there is power there is money; where there is money there is corruption. As John Dalberg Acton, first Baron Acton, said, 'Power corrupts and absolute power corrupts absolutely.' Without power nothing would move or change. Dockyard shipwright Jimmy Mactavish, General Secretary of the Workers' Educational Association, fought against the council's corruption. The Victorian age was dominated by coal and steam. In the twentieth century, local government reorganisation produced a regional development plan for the South East, placing new obligations on the city council. Massive population growth was coming, along with new job and housing requirements.

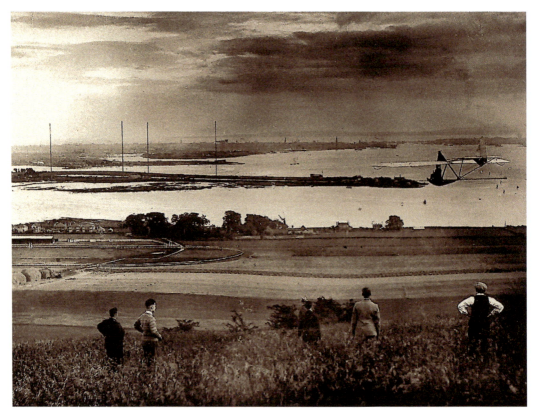

Portsmouth was home to distinguished aeronautical engineer and author Nevil Shute. This 1919 image pre-dates his arrival, the flyer having no engine, but gliding over Portsdown Hill. All is changed now. Portsdown Park Housing development and the Farlington bypass section of the M275 cost £2.5 million. (*Portsmouth News*)

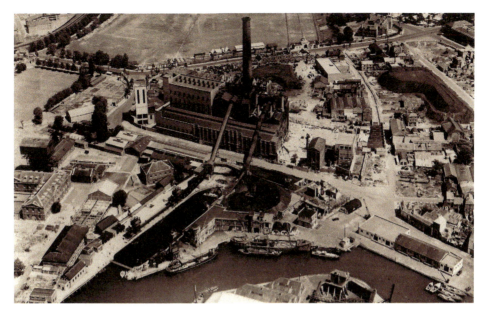

Portsmouth Power Station is the centrepiece of this war-weary image, 12 June 1949. Fittingly, in a society that worships power and output more than God, it occupied the site of a medieval church. The power station opened here, the nation's first municipal power station, near Camber Dock where colliers delivered via giant conveyor belts. Landport Gate marks the entrance to United Services Ground. (Simmons Aerofilms)

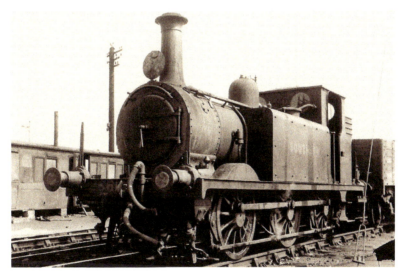

Class AIX 0-6-0 'Terrier' tank engine at Fratton Engine depot and marshalling yards, 16 August 1947. The Southern Railway livery would soon be replaced by British Railways logos and black livery, following the Labour government's nationalisation of the British rail network. This tiny Victorian-designed engine pulled mixed traffic and big coaches on the famous 4½-mile Havant to Hayling line, which sadly closed in 1963, adding to massive road congestion as the island developed. Road builder (Marples Ridgeway) and Transport Minister Ernest Marples set out to use his friend Dr Beeching to cut as many rail miles as possible. He sacked Beeching for not going far enough. (R. J. Buckley/Initial Photographics)

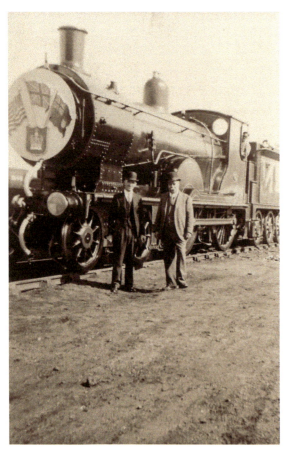

Left: 'Scotty' Johnson with the T9 4-4-0 (these numbers refer to the wheel axle arrangement, here four small wheels and four large ones). It is decked out ready to pick up the royal train at Fratton in 1936. Alfie Downs was a Guildford driver. Both men wear the traditional bowler hat. (George Elliot)

Below: Tory wartime prime minister Winston Churchill led the war effort, and was surprised when the nation rejected him in peace. Commoners were offered rewards for their sacrifice. So came the nationalisation of strategic industry and creation of the NHS. Railways were run down. Almost bankrupt and in debt to America, which gave money to Germany to stop communism, Britain found the means to take them over. So here are two class H2 4-4-2 locomotives, *South Foreland* 32421 alongside *Trevose Head* 32425, both in the new British Railways livery at Fratton, 5 May 1953. (B. K. B. Green/Initial Photographics)

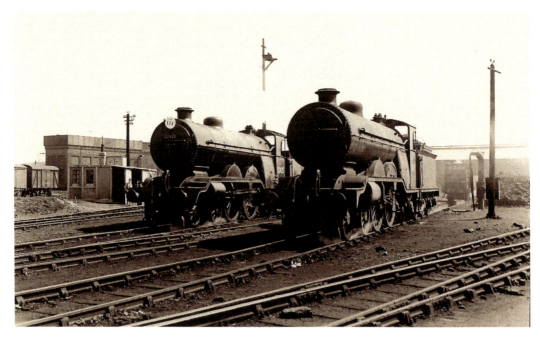

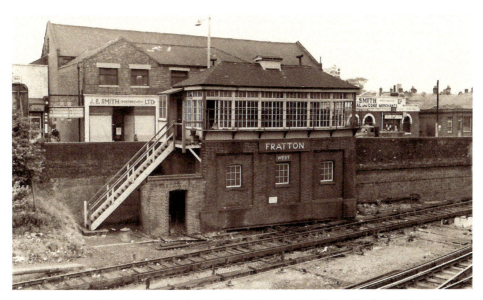

Fratton West signal box was made redundant by 1960s new signalling technology. This is the scene on 14 June 1967. Steam and coal still had importance, as J. E. Smith's premises and the parked coal lorry on Goldsmith Avenue attest in the background. These buildings lingered on into the early 2000s, but have been replaced by luxury flats. The station on the London and Brighton South Coast Railway was opened on 1 July 1885, serving as an interchange with the short-lived Southsea railway branch line, which followed the curve of the now Goldsmith Avenue. (Edwin Wilmshurst)

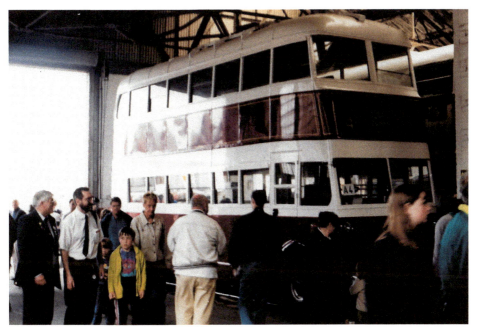

This preserved 1934 Portsmouth Corporation AEC trolleybus was photographed at the city's last bus rally in July 2000. The event, on the common, was forced to close because of health and safety concerns. The bus preservation society was forced by the corporation to vacate their large shed in Broad Street to make way for redevelopment.

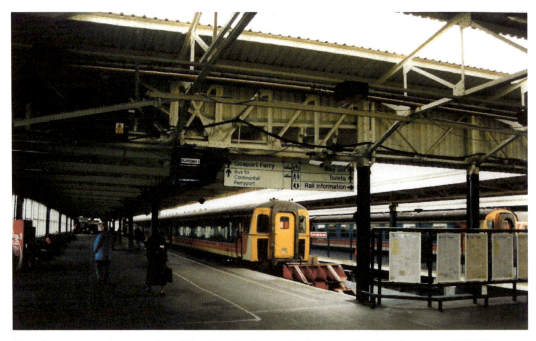

Slam door trains at Portsmouth and Southsea Station on the Portsmouth to London route, 1998. The following year, railway companies were ordered to phase them out by 2005.

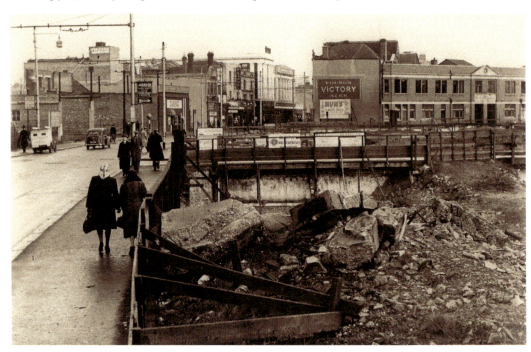

Portsmouth City Centre Northern Quarter, *c.* 1948, where the Tricorn would eventually overwhelm. Alec Coleman submitted the unusual plans drawn up by the Owen Luder Partnership with Rodney Gordon. Heavy bombing took a massive toll here as Luftwaffe pilots dropped bombs just short of the neighbouring dockyard. A few old landmarks remain here in spite of the deluge. (Portsmouth City Museum)

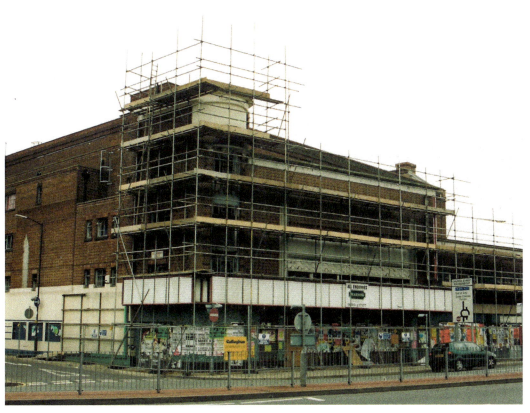

Demolition of the ABC (formerly the Savoy) in Commercial Road, March 2002. The 1,900-seater cinema opened in July 1937, with Reginald Porter Brown rising up through the floor on his Crompton Wonder Organ. Television became popular in the 1950s as cinema audiences declined, with almost forty picture houses closing locally. The Savoy closed, but reopened as the ABC in 1964, then closing again in 1999. Meanwhile a new 2,800-seater eleven-screen cinema has opened at Gunwharf Quays as cinema offers an overwhelming world of sound, light, drama and escape.

Demolition requires the power of money. Centros Miller representatives are seen here with development plans for the old Tricorn site in 2004. The city was experiencing more dockyard and naval cuts. The economy needed boosting. The university needed to attract a wide range of students to a modern city.

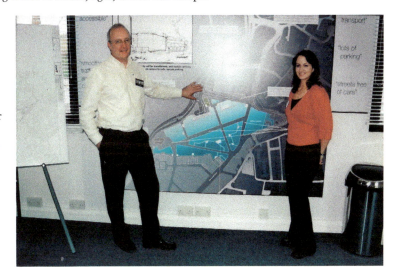

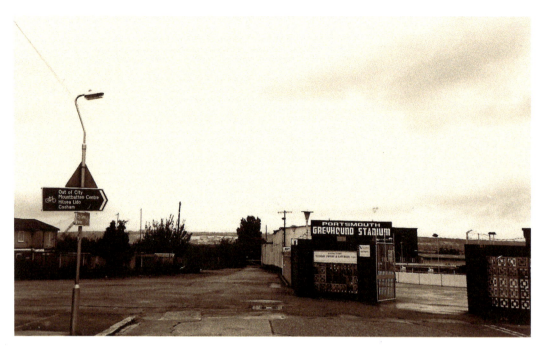

The Tipner Greyhound Track, 1999. Dog racing was a working man's sport. Portsmouth's first track in Copnor closed owing to flooding. The following year, 1931, the council offered a new 8-acre site in Tipner – the old Stamshaw Chemical company works. The sport declined and the stadium closed on 27 March 2010. Over the years it became so vandalised there was nothing left.

9

Byways

Post-war planners looked towards a more orderly and efficient future. Success is debatable. The old days had Thomas Ellis Owen building fine houses and churches. But most growth was high-density terraces, with those surviving now costing a fortune. The old days were rather more meandering but under the iron grip of class rule. Looking back, old sights in pictures conjure up old sounds, but one mustn't overuse the rose-tinted spectacles when looking at the old ways and byways.

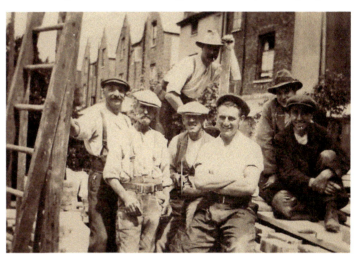

Hoad's craftsmen working on 187 Eastfield Road, Southsea, 1933. Portsmouth had an abundance of highly skilled craftsmen thanks to the Royal Dockyard apprenticeship scheme. (John Mason)

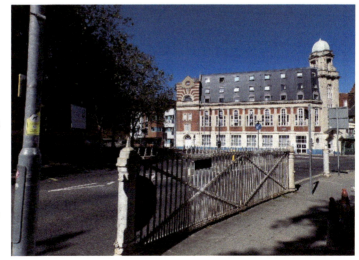

The plaque on this disused level crossing gate says, 'This gate and posts are relics of the old dockyard railway link that used to pass over Edinburgh Road.' The track was completed in 1846 and used until 1977. The line was dismantled during the 1980s to allow for landscaping along Unicorn Road. The building in the background is Portsmouth's original advanced technology college, from which the polytechnic and university developed.

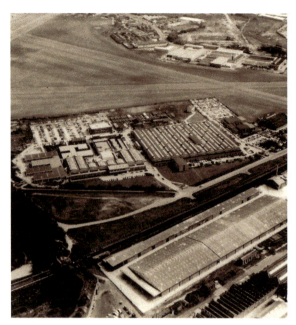

Portsmouth Airport, late 1970s. Nevil Shute Norway brought his Airspeed Company to Portsmouth Airport in the 1930s because of the city's enlightened corporation and expanding industrial facilities at the airport. Albert Road news vendor and tobacconist H. E. King told Robert Cook: 'Security was very lax during the 1930s. with German flyers landing at the airport, being given great hospitality and allowed to snoop around.' The old grass runway was the airport's downfall. Two Channel Airways turboprop aircraft overshot the runway, veering on to Eastern Road, on 15 August 1967. Another interesting feature of this photograph is the railway line passing under the old ramparts, which were part of the city's massive old defences. (Simmons Aerofilms)

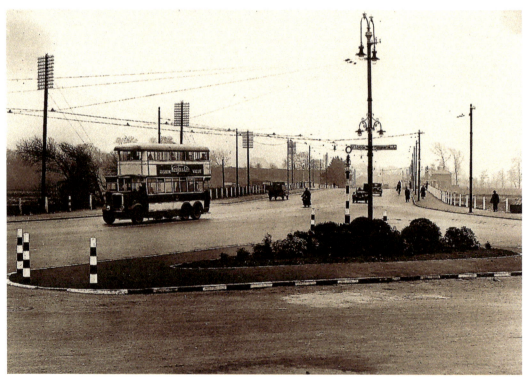

A Portsmouth Corporation Karrier WL6 bus, advertising Knight & Lee's Store. Here the bus passes the junction of London Road and Southampton Road, Hilsea. The old defensive ramparts are in the distance. Retired police sergeant Eddie Wallace recalled having to note the numbers of cars crossing the bridge late at night. It would be impossible and unnecessary to do that now, in the age of security cameras. (*Portsmouth News*)

Right: Youth unemployment is still a big issue. This is the Juvenile Employment Bureau, Victoria Road North, at the junction of Sydenham Terrace with Fratton Road, 1935. The service was started to help youngsters find employment during the 1930s depression years. Now it has gone, and the site is part of a big roundabout and Winston Churchill Avenue. (*Portsmouth News*)

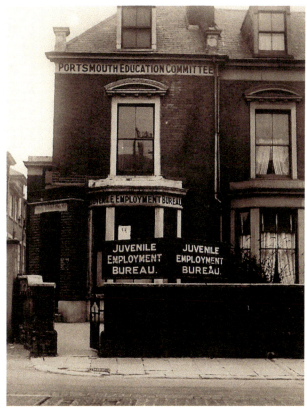

Below: Buckingham House, *c.* 1912. The Villiers were self-indulgent ruthless spendthrifts. So it was no surprise when the king's favourite and Duke of Buckingham (hence Buckingham Palace) met a bloody end at the hands of apparently mad soldier John Felton in this house, owned by Captain John Mason and then called the Spotted Dog. The duke had been in town planning the relief of La Rochelle, but owed his mercenaries pay, so was stabbed as he was about to leave.

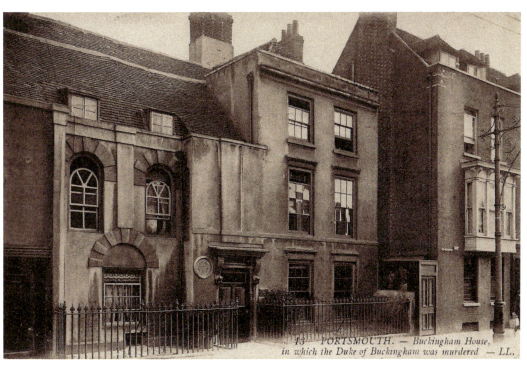

75

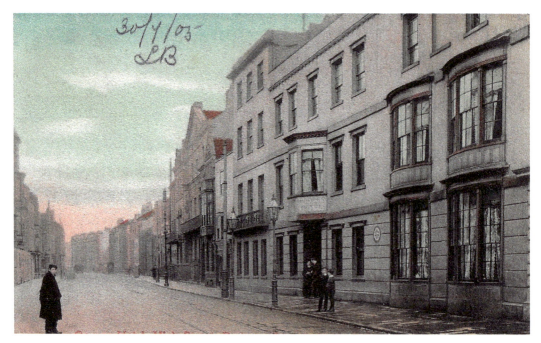

George Hotel, High Street, Old Portsmouth, 1905. It isn't certain whether Admiral Lord Horatio Nelson spent his last night here, but he did take his last breakfast here before setting off for the Battle of Trafalgar. He left via the back door into Penny Street, where adoring crowds cheered that he had their hearts. The hotel was destroyed by wartime bombs.

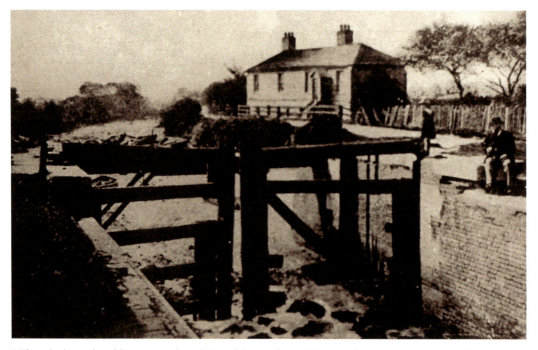

Milton lock on the old Portsmouth and Arundel Canal, *c.* 1910. Canals were made obsolete by the railways. Parts of the canal bed were sold to the Chichester to Portsmouth branch railway.

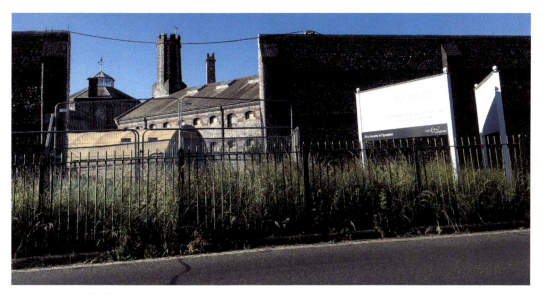

Portsmouth's Victorian Kingston Prison, built in 1877, was deemed not fit for purpose in 2002. Built to a radial design, it was housing long-term and death sentence prisoners after the Second World War – when it had served as a police station. Up until closure in 2013, it had been housing elderly with life sentences. Photographed here in March 2019, the hoarding was advertising luxury apartments.

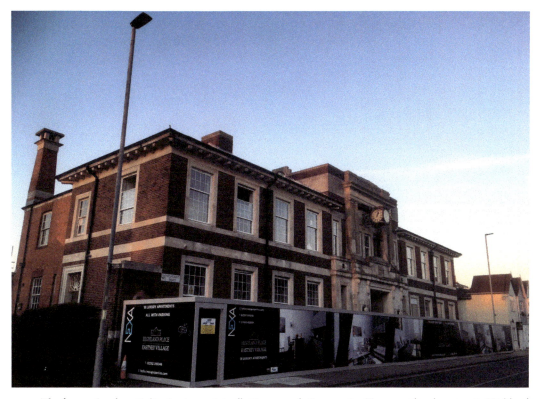

The former Southsea Police Station, originally Portsmouth Corporation Transport headquarters in Highland Road. It was closed to the public in 2013, and is shown here being developed into more luxury flats.

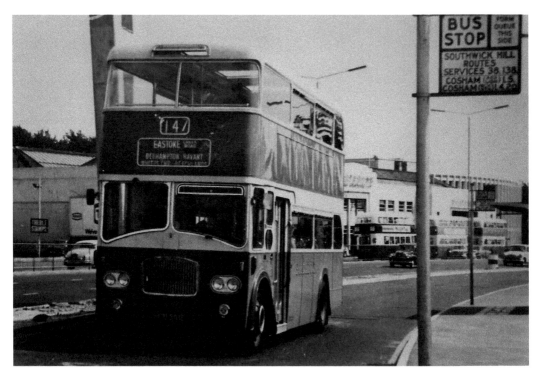

Like the Southdown Leyland bus in this 1960s image, the Southdown Bus Garage at Hilsea, in the background, has long gone following Thatcher's big sell-off of the National Bus Company and deregulation. (Dave Brunnen)

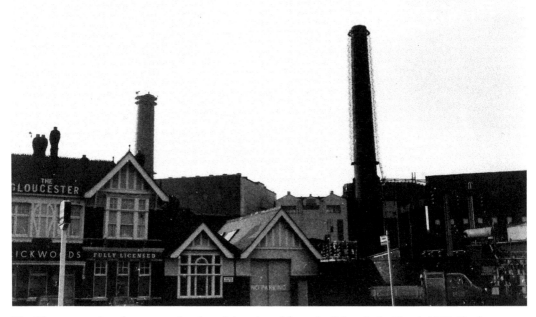

The Gloucester pub and power station demolition viewed from the Polytechnic, March 1982. (Andrew Marshall)

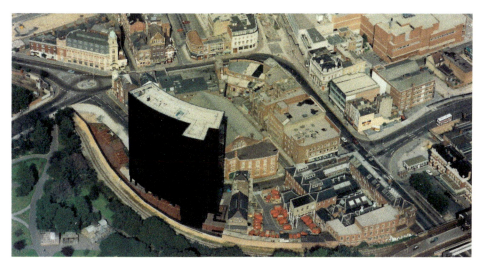

Opened in 1973, this was Zurich House in 1977, where R. J. Cook did a spell in the post room; he recalls it being air conditioned with all mod cons. Abandoned for eight years after Zurich Insurance moved to a bleak industrial estate in Fareham, it is now owned by the Student Housing Company and is home to 1,000 students in its fourteen-storey tower. The steel had begun to decarbonate, one reason why restoration cost £51 million. We also see the doomed dockyard railway curving past the large Post Office, the old College of Advanced Technology, also converted to student residences, and the Trafalgar Institute. (Simmons Aerofilms)

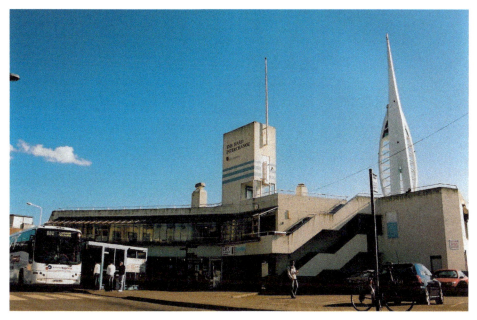

The old Portsmouth Hard Interchange before redevelopment. The new interchange opened in March 2017. It costs £2 million as part of a £1.8 billion investment programme to improve the city's infrastructure. However, it has been sinking since, costing a fortune in running repairs. This is a multi-modal transport hub which aims to improve the infrastructure and transport links into the city. It forms a new high-quality gateway to one of the busiest parts of Portsmouth. There are 13 million visitors a year. The new interchange was to complete the southern end of the Park and Ride network.

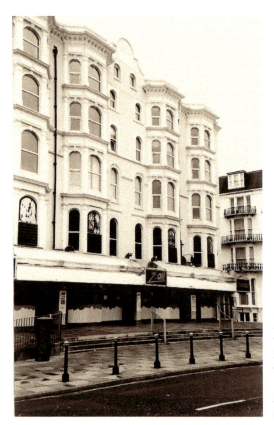

Left: The two nightclubs here are Zoom, which R. J. Cook recalls as 'Neroes', and the infamous Joanna's. Zoom became Envy, and the whole building was demolished in 2008.

Below: The long-gone Knight & Lee's department store in Palmerston Road, 1999.

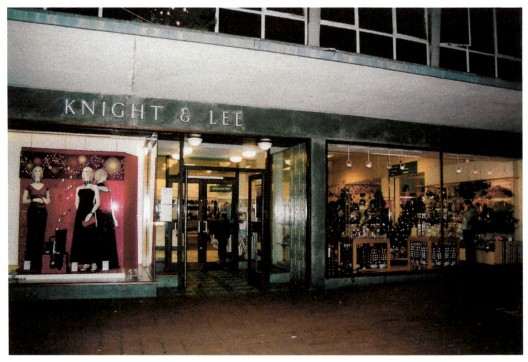

10
Community

A community is a group of people living in close proximity who have cultural and religious or other characteristics in common. To many locals, this is Portsmouth's greatest loss. Sociologists have their definitions of community, and politicians have aspired to create them, but they are very much a state of mind, needing constant reference points.

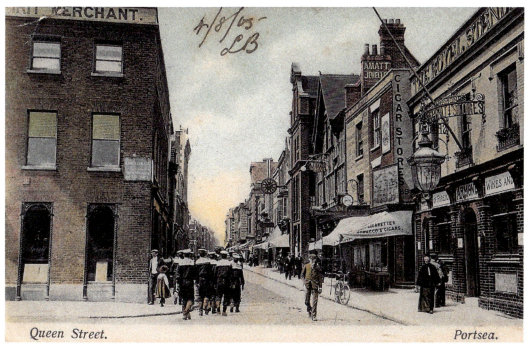

Queen Street, Portsea, looking towards the Hard from the junction with Lion Terrace, *c.* 1905. Sailors weren't shy about being around town in uniform in those days. Wine and cigars are advertised, and fever, garrison and women's hospitals are out of sight along Lion Terrace.

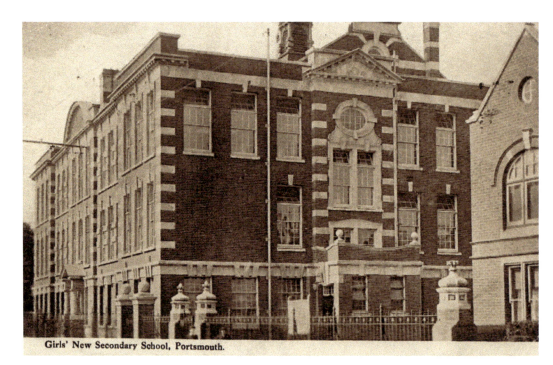

Girls' New Secondary School, Portsmouth.

The girls' new secondary school just after opening in 1907. The building is still there, but its purpose has changed. Girls are not taught separately any more, and this one is now The Priory.

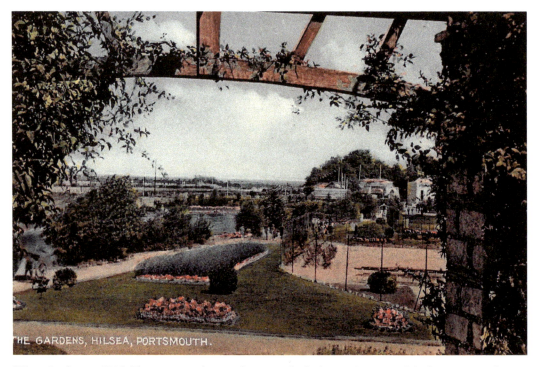

THE GARDENS, HILSEA, PORTSMOUTH.

Hilsea Gardens, *c.* 1905. There was much room for nature back then, as Portsmouth had yet to expand north across the water.

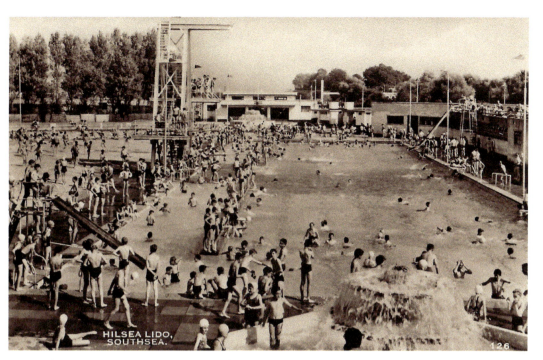

A hot day at Hilsea Lido, just south of Port Creek, 1955. Plans to restore and reopen this in 2002, spending £1 million, did not come to pass.

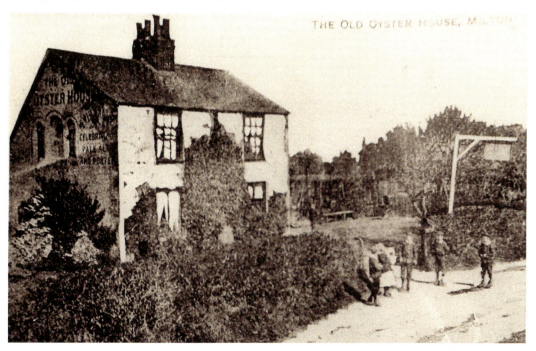

The Oyster House, Common Lane, *c.* 1912. Keen ramblers could relax here after walking from the canal basin in the town centre. The building was replaced with a new and modern pub called The Old Oyster House. (Sue Bray)

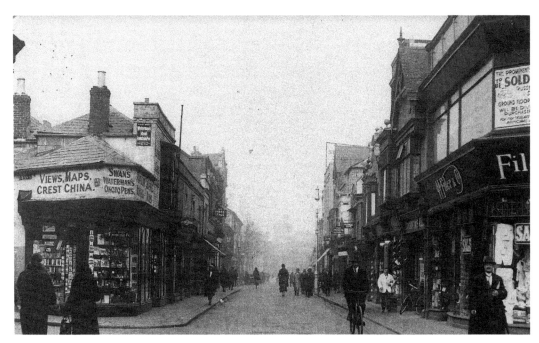

Russell Street looking towards the Guildhall at the junction with Swan Street, mid-1930s. Kathy Chard recalls her parents buying glassware for their pub, the Brewery Tap, in this street. A keen pianist, she remembers buying music in a shop near here. (Portsmouth City Museum)

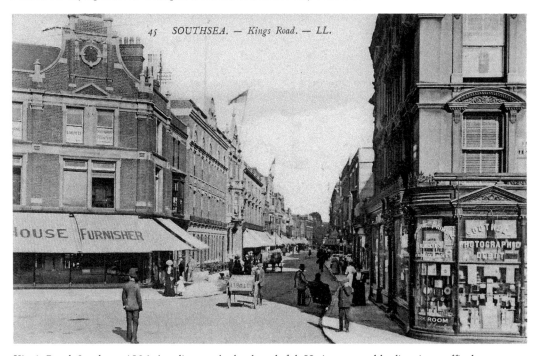

King's Road, Southsea, 1906. A policeman looks thoughtful. He is presumably directing traffic, heavy even in the horse and cart age. Wiped out by wartime bombs, this is no longer a thriving retail area. The scene is now dominated by a roundabout.

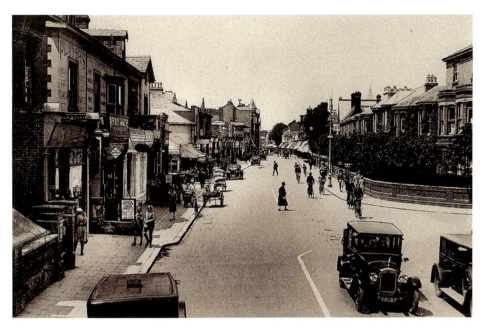

Elm Grove looking towards King's Avenue near the junction with Victoria Road. Shop blinds attest to the area's commercial importance. (*Portsmouth News*)

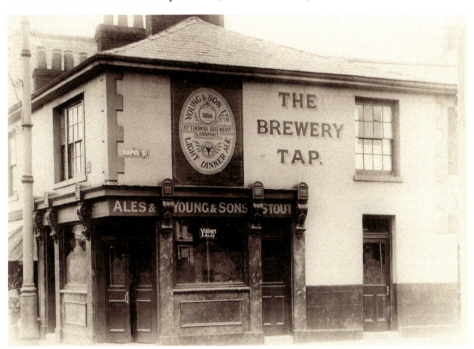

George Whateley's Brewery Tap pub in Chapel Street, early 1900s. Kathy Chard grew up in this pub. The greengrocer kept his horse and cart on neighbouring spare ground. Her dad said she wouldn't need a job when she left school. Kathy said: 'It seems terrible to say it, but I had a good war. It got me out of the pub. I enjoyed working in the dockyard. When the sirens went I sat in number 18 store.' (Kathy Chard)

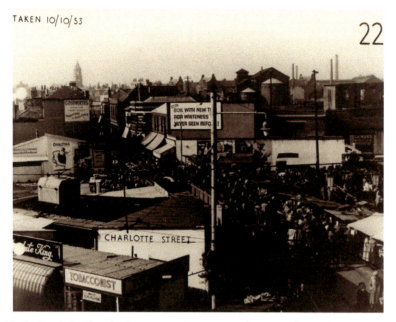

The redoubtable St Agatha's Church gives us our bearings in this scene from Charlotte Street, early 1950s. No doubt the Luftwaffe spared the church as a useful landmark when they were aiming for the nearby dockyard. (Portsmouth City Museum)

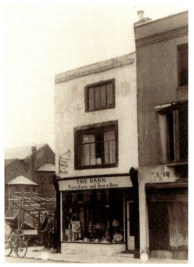 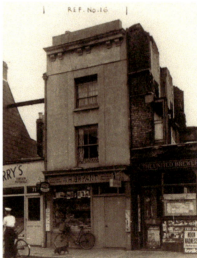

Above left: Charlotte Street, between Amelia Street and Alfred Street, 1950s. St Agatha's Church is still going strong in this picture. (Portsmouth City Museum)

Above right: Charlotte Street, early 1950s. This picture shows numbers 71 to 75. Bicycles and sailors were everyday sights in the 1940s to the 1960s. The United Brewery went years ago, along with everything else here. Bryant's window has pictures of pop stars in it and a chewing gum dispenser on the front wall. These were the little shops that brought people together. Across the road a whole community had been devastated by the Blitz. Alec Coleman and Owen Luder would soon be here with new ideas about retailing. Housing policy was changing too. (Portsmouth City Museum)

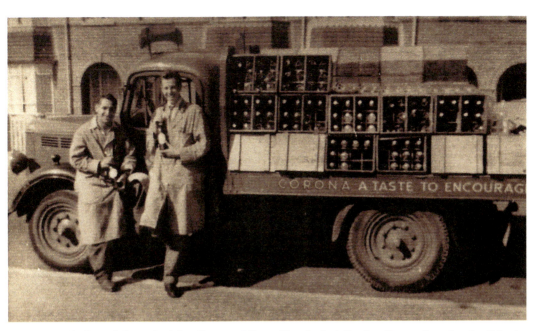

Ernest Habens, left, worked for all sorts of firms. Here he is delivering Corona (not the virus!) in the early 1950s. Corona made different flavours of lemonade in King's Street, Southsea. 'I had a regular round,' Ernest said. He was rehoused to Paulsgrove after the war. 'Many people had no idea what baths were for and stored coal in them.' (Ernest Habens)

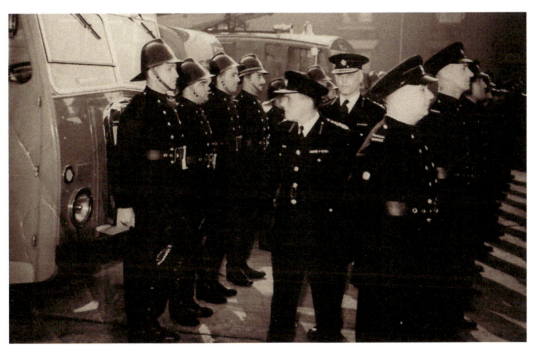

Portsmouth firemen are inspected at Copnor, 1950s. Fire crews were subject to military-style discipline. Pre-war, all trainee police, fire and ambulance crews had to serve a period in all services before specialising. (Harold Atwell)

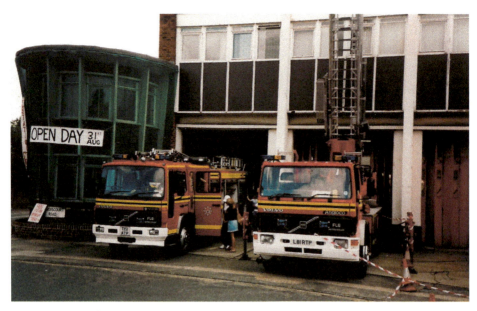

Copnor Fire Station open day, 2002. Originally Portsmouth Fire Service headquarters, it was closed in 2008: equipment and crews were redeployed to Cosham, Southsea and Havant. The site has been redeveloped for retirement flats.

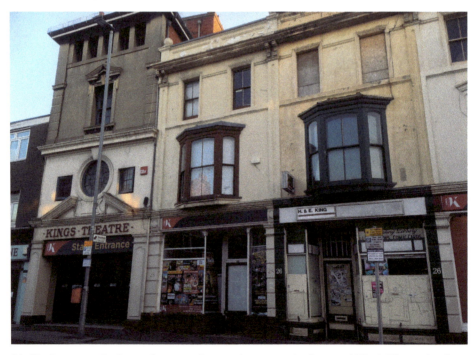

Mr King's news and tobacco shop next door to the appropriately named King's Theatre has been closed for many years. R. J. Cook remembers Mr King as rather eccentric, insisting that Eisenhower and 'Monty' used the upstairs front room to part-plan D-Day. He had a number of large portrait photos of wartime service men and women on his wall, and insisted that there was still an unexploded bomb in the equally eccentric Albert Road, where he was a perfect fit for many years.

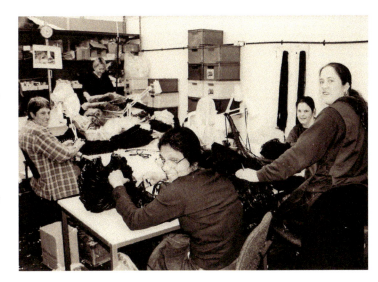

Skilled workers at the Gemini foundation garment factory, Fratton, 1999. The company was making garments for leading brands such as Agent Provocateur when this picture was taken. Corsetry was a long-established industry, with firms such as Vollers and Leethems, in Portsmouth, but modern lifestyles have reduced demand.

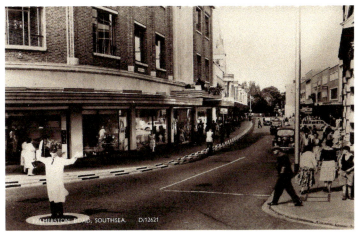

Palmerston Road, in a thriving retail area, viewed from Castle Drive, at a point known colloquially as Handley's Corner. Police are very different now, in a different world. The two major stores are closed and there is talk of a £7 million residential development in what was once a premier Southsea retail area.

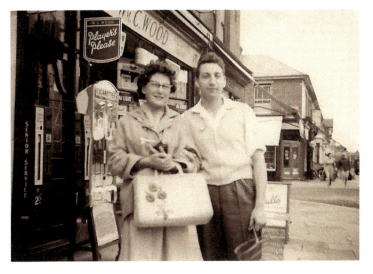

Newlyweds Shirley and Ivan Warne outside the newsagents in Francis Avenue, 1959. They had just bought their house in nearby Percy Road.

89

11

Where Now?

Since the 1980s, we have seen manufacturing and engineering decline across the country, which has had a big impact locally. Defence cuts have withered the dockyard and Britain no longer leads the world in shipbuilding. The Victorian age of coal, steam and high hopes has passed. We were told in the 1980s that the future was hi-tech, information and services. With the impact of Covid-19 lockdowns, we are being told to welcome a new norm. Who really knows what that will be in an increasingly unstable world of new wars and mass movements of people. Portsmouth has placed high hopes on education and the university.

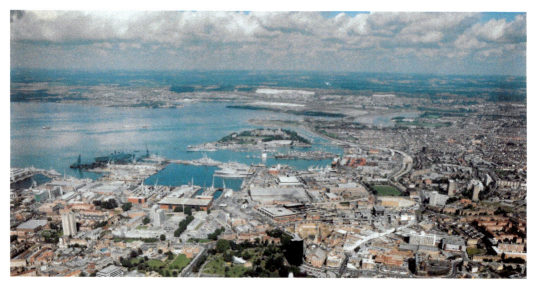

This late 1970s view northward across the dockyard shows us the scar of the M275, cutting across reclaimed land. It led to many homes demolished in the old Derby Road red light area and Ranleigh Road. The traffic has today caught up and is overwhelming at peak periods. There is also the scar where the Royal Portsmouth Hospital used to be, demolished in March 1979. The NHS was rationalising in the Thatcher era: St James' Hospital also closed, with Queen Alexandra expanding. (Simmons Aerofilms)

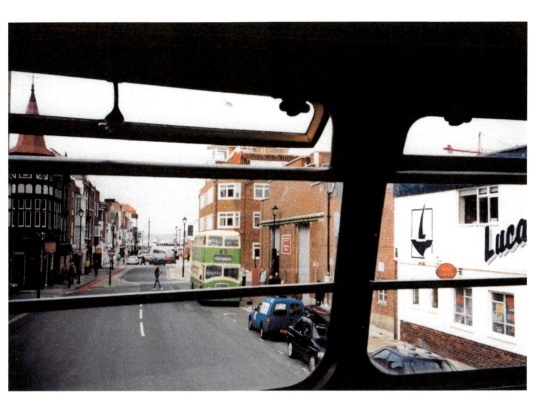

Above: R. J. Cook atop a vintage Leyland PD3, formerly of Southdown, approaching the Preservation Society's premises in Broad Street, summer 2000. Another PD3 approaches from the other direction en route to the common.

Right: Admiralty House, University Student residence, Queen Street, February 2019. The nearby dockyard has contracted massively, with a short-lived BAE Systems revival of shipbuilding activities ended, but the student population has expanded massively to over 31,000 with 3,500 staff. There are 5,200 students from 150 different countries.

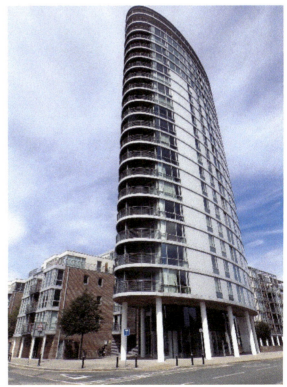

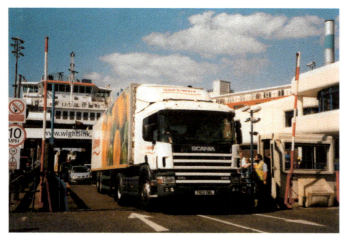

A Safeway class one truck disembarks from the Isle of Wight ferry in the summer of 1999. Safeway has gone, and the ferry company has a new environmentally friendly ship, built in Turkey.

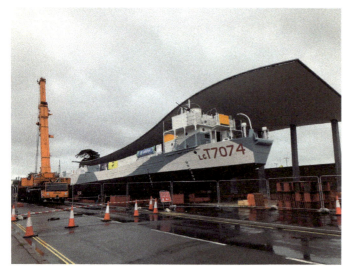

Landing craft T7074, restored by dockyard apprentices after discovery in the Thames Estuary, is here being moved into a purpose-built display facility at the D-Day museum on a stormy Thursday afternoon, 7 August 2020.

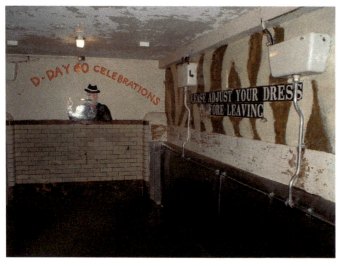

An interesting D-Day celebratory mural in the public toilets near Clarence Pier, 2004.

Mr Butch's shop, Charlotte Street, 1998. Family butchers have struggled to compete with supermarkets. The Revd Mr Dolling, in his memoir of ten years working in a Portsmouth slum, observed that there were so many butchers in this street, and the slaughterhouses behind, that it was colloquially known as Bloody Row.

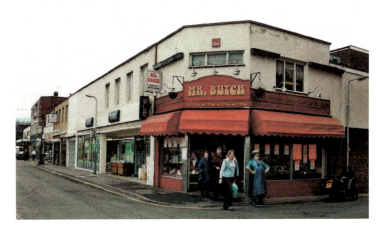

Fratton Park football ground the day Portsmouth was promoted to the Premier League. A supporter from the 1980s told of the exciting days of club supporters fighting each other, and the feeling of sickness he had in anticipation the morning before.

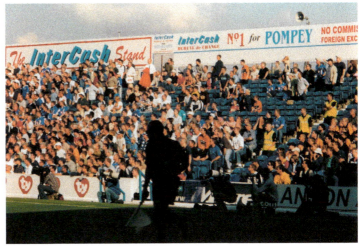

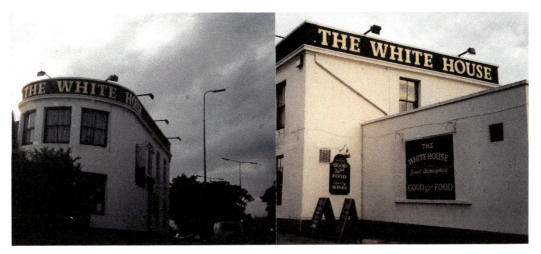

The White House public house, Milton Road, 1990. Pubs are struggling. Conversion to restaurants was one way to survive, but lockdown leaves many on the brink.

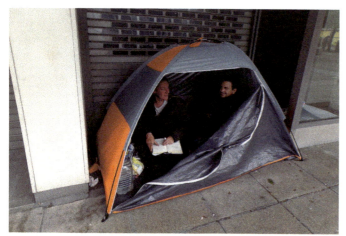

Two old schoolmates, homeless, camped out in Arundel Street, March 2018. It was a cold day. When the council warden came along, the photographer was warned that taking pictures of them being moved on would lead to police action.

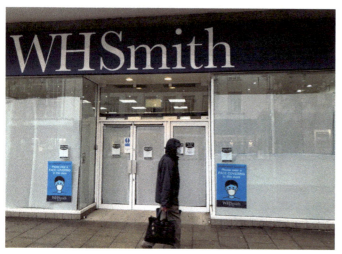

Covid-19 lockdowns have had a terrible impact on trade and jobs. Here is WHSmith in Commercial Road, 2 August 2020. Notices announce permanent closure. Dockyard employment shrank massively from a 26,000 peak in 1950. The university, with its transitory population, has not taken up the slack.

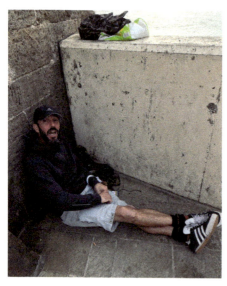

Liverpudlian John, ex-sailor and soldier, back in Old Portsmouth in summer 2018, his favourite place in England. He was having help with PTSD, and is seen here relaxing in a cul-de-sac by the old defensive walls that once thronged with prostitutes.

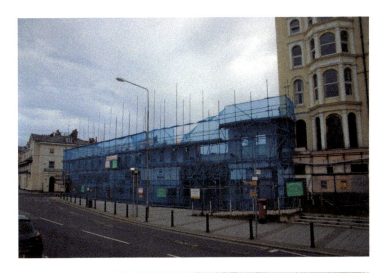

Nero's and Joanna's, infamous Southsea nightclubs, being demolished, summer 2008. Joanna's was a rough house favoured by young drunken sailors looking for 'love'. Nero's was a little more refined. The naval provost's little blue Bedford CA vans were always waiting near the South Parade Pier when the clubs turned out, according to R. J. Cook.

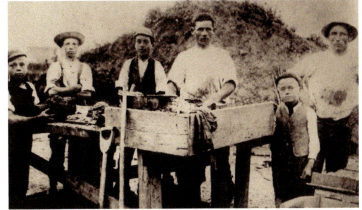

The Pycroft family hand-making bricks, early 1900s. Portsmouth and Southsea had an insatiable demand for bricks. (Noel Pycroft)

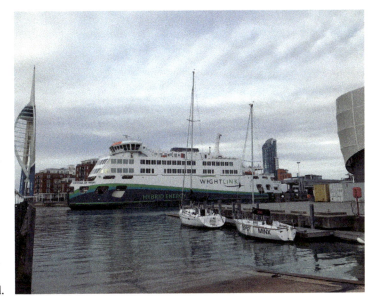

Wightlink's new £45 million 2,500-ton Turkish flagship *Victoria* prepares to dock on a stormy night in February 2020. Chief Executive Keith Greenfield said the ship, which carries 158 cars, will improve comfort and service, with more freight being carried to the island.

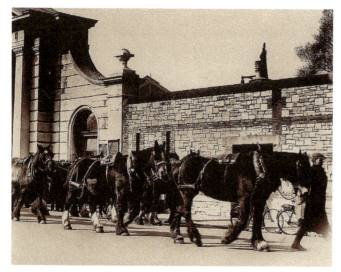

A Saturday in March 1933, the year Hitler came to power, with dockyard horses being led to the stables for a relaxing weekend. Horsepower was ubiquitous before the war, then faded away except for sport and relaxation.

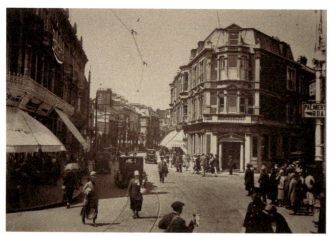

The Junction of Osborne and Portland Roads, Southsea, 1920s. Note tram wires. How we perceive loss depends on one's point of view. To some, loss is gain, the absence of change being seen as stagnation. However, people may struggle to keep up, and Covid-19 lockdowns put a new perspective on what is lost.

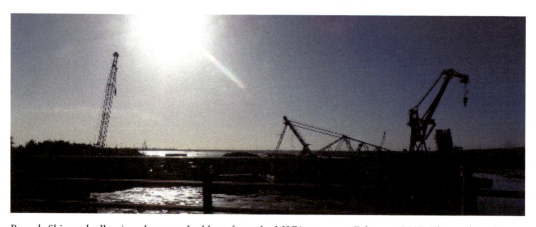

Pounds Shipyard, all quiet, photographed here from the M271 at sunset, February 2020. The yard used to be busy breaking up the Navy's old ships and submarines. Now the work goes to Turkey.